Lecture Notes in Computer Science 4406

Commenced Publication in 1973
Founding and Former Series Editors:
Gerhard Goos, Juris Hartmanis, and Jan van Leeuwen

T0223142

Wolfgang De Meuter (Ed.)

Advances in Smalltalk

14th International Smalltalk Conference, ISC 2006
Prague, Czech Republic, September 4-8, 2006
Revised Selected Papers

 Springer

Volume Editor

Wolfgang De Meuter
Programming Technology Laboratory
Vrije Universiteit Brussel
Belgium
E-mail: wdmeuter@vub.ac.be

Library of Congress Control Number: 2007923851

CR Subject Classification (1998): D.1, D.2, D.3, F.3

LNCS Sublibrary: SL 2 – Programming and Software Engineering

ISSN   0302-9743
ISBN-10   3-540-71835-4 Springer Berlin Heidelberg New York
ISBN-13   978-3-540-71835-2 Springer Berlin Heidelberg New York

Springer is a part of Springer Science+Business Media

springer.com

© Springer-Verlag Berlin Heidelberg 2007
Printed in Germany

Typesetting: Camera-ready by author, data conversion by Scientific Publishing Services, Chennai, India
Printed on acid-free paper   SPIN: 12044788   06/3180   5 4 3 2 1 0

Preface

The 14th International Smalltalk Conference took place in the first week of September 2006 in Prague, Czech Republic. This volume contains the peer-reviewed technical papers that were presented during the academic track of the conference.

The International Smalltalk Conference evolved out of the annual meeting of the European Smalltalk User Group (ESUG). This meeting usually lasts about a week and allows Smalltalk experts to discuss Smalltalk solutions and environments. The meeting attracts a diverse audience consisting of Smalltalkers from industry as well as from academia. Thanks to the perpetual effort of people like Stéphane Ducasse, Noury Bouraqadi, Serge Stinckwich and Roel Wuyts, over the years the ESUG meeting was provided with a separate academic research track during which researchers could present academic results about Smalltalk and its development tools. Unfortunately, no formal publication forum was associated with this track, which made it less attractive for authors to submit a paper. Starting with this edition of the conference, we hope this will change. An agreement was reached with Springer to publish a post-conference proceedings of this 14th edition. I think our community owes a big thank you to Stéphane for this! Hopefully next year this agreement can evolve into a 15th edition of the conference with formally announced proceedings. This will certainly motivate more Smalltalk researchers to submit a paper!

The conference accepted just over half of the submissions. Although this can be interpreted as a sign of low quality, I think it is not. The set of researchers conducting their research in Smalltalk is quite small. However, as is the case with the code produced by Smalltalkers, the quality-to-quantity ratio of the research is high. This is confirmed by the fact that all papers were reviewed by at least three members of the international Program Committee. The committee consisted of a number of researchers that are highly renowned in the field of object-oriented programming in general and in the Smalltalk world in particular. I would like to thank them for their efforts in trying to make this a conference of outstanding quality.

September 2006   Wolfgang De Meuter

Organization

Program Committee

Dave Simmons, Smallscript Corporation, USA
Noury Bouraqadi, Ecole des Mines de Douai, France
Nathanael Schaerli, Google R&D, Zurich, Switzerland
Andrew Black, Portland State University, USA
Serge Stinckwich, Université de Caen, France
Joseph Pelrine, MetaProg GmbH, Switzerland
Alan Knight, Cincom, USA
Thomas Kuehne, Technische Universität Darmstadt, Germany
Christophe Roche, Université de Savoie, France
Maja D'Hondt, Université des Sciences et Technologies de Lille, France
Maximo Prieto, Universidad Nacional de La Plata, Argentina
Brian Foote University of Illinois at Urbana-Champaign, USA
Dave Thomas, Bedarra Research Labs, USA
Gilad Bracha, SUN Java Software, USA
Serge Demeyer, Universiteit Antwerpen, Belgium
Pierre Cointe, Ecole de Mines de Nantes, France
Michel Tillman, Real Software, Belgium
Tudor Girba, Universität Bern, Switzerland

Table of Contents

Application-Specific Models and Pointcuts Using a Logic Meta
Language 1
    Johan Brichau, Andy Kellens, Kris Gybels, Kim Mens,
    Robert Hirschfeld, and Theo D'Hondt

An Object-Oriented Approach for Context-Aware Applications 23
    Andrés Fortier, Nicolás Cañibano, Julián Grigera,
    Gustavo Rossi, and Silvia Gordillo

Unanticipated Partial Behavioral Reflection 47
    David Röthlisberger, Marcus Denker, and Éric Tanter

Stateful Traits 66
    Alexandre Bergel, Stéphane Ducasse, Oscar Nierstrasz, and
    Roel Wuyts

SCL: A Simple, Uniform and Operational Language for
Component-Oriented Programming in Smalltalk 91
    Luc Fabresse, Christophe Dony, and Marianne Huchard

Let's Modularize the Data Model Specifications of the ObjectLens in
VisualWorks/Smalltalk 111
    Michael Prasse

Meta-driven Browsers 134
    Alexandre Bergel, Stéphane Ducasse, Colin Putney, and Roel Wuyts

Author Index 157

Application-Specific Models and Pointcuts Using a Logic Meta Language

Johan Brichau[2,3,*], Andy Kellens[1,**], Kris Gybels[1], Kim Mens[2], Robert Hirschfeld[4], and Theo D'Hondt[1]

[1] Programming Technology Lab
Vrije Universiteit Brussel, Belgium
{akellens,kris.gybels,tjdhondt}@vub.ac.be
[2] Département d'Ingénierie Informatique
Université catholique de Louvain, Belgium
{johan.brichau,kim.mens}@uclouvain.be
[3] Laboratoire d'Informatique Fondamentale de Lille
Université des Sciences et Technologies de Lille, France
[4] Hasso-Plattner-Institut
Potsdam, Germany
hirschfeld@hpi.uni-potsdam.de

Abstract. In contemporary aspect-oriented languages, pointcuts are usually specified directly in terms of the structure of the source code. The definition of such low-level pointcuts requires aspect developers to have a profound understanding of the entire application's implementation and often leads to complex, fragile, and hard to maintain pointcut definitions. To resolve these issues, we present an aspect-oriented programming system that features a logic-based pointcut language that is open such that it can be extended with application-specific pointcut predicates. These predicates define an application-specific model that serves as a contract that base-program developers provide and aspect developers can depend upon. As a result, pointcuts can be specified in terms of this more high-level model of the application which confines all intricate implementation details that are otherwise exposed in the pointcut definitions themselves.

1 Introduction

Aspect-oriented Software Development (AOSD) is a recent, yet established development paradigm that enhances existing development paradigms with advanced encapsulation and modularisation capabilities [1,2]. In particular, aspect-oriented programming languages provide a new kind of abstraction, called *aspect*, that allows a developer to modularise the implementation of crosscutting concerns such

---

* This work was partially supported by the European Network of Excellence AOSD-Europe.
** Ph.D. scholarship funded by the "Institute for the Promotion of Innovation through Science and Technology in Flanders" (IWT Vlaanderen).

W. De Meuter (Ed.): ISC 2006, LNCS 4406, pp. 1–22, 2007.

as synchronisation, transaction management, exception handling, etc. Such concerns are traditionally spread across various modules in the implementation, causing tangled and scattered code [3]. The improved modularity and separation of concerns [4], that can be achieved using aspects, intends not only to aid initial development, but also to allow developers to better manage software complexity, evolution and reuse.

One of the most essential characteristics of an aspect-oriented programming language is that aspects are not *explicitly* invoked but instead, are *implicitly* invoked [5]. This has also been referred to as the 'obliviousness' property of aspect orientation [6]. It means that the *base program* (i.e., the program without the aspects) does not explicitly invoke the aspects because the aspects themselves specify when and where they need to be invoked by means of a *pointcut definition*. A pointcut essentially specifies a set of *join points*, which are specific points in the base program where the aspect will be invoked implicitly. Such a pointcut definition typically relies on structural and behavioural properties of the base program to express the intended join points. For example, if an aspect must be triggered at the instantiation of each new object of a particular class, its pointcut must capture those join points whose properties correspond with the execution of the constructor method. As a result, each time the constructor method is executed (i.e. an instance is created), the aspect is invoked. In most aspect languages, this corresponds to the execution of an *advice*, which is a sequence of instructions executed before, after or around the execution of the join point.

Unfortunately, in many cases, defining and maintaining an appropriate pointcut is a rather complex activity. First of all, an aspect developer must carefully analyse and understand the structure of the entire application and the properties shared by all intended join points in particular. Some of these properties can be directly tied to abstractions that are available in the programming language but other properties are based on programming conventions such as naming schemes. 'Object instantiation' join points, for example, can be identified as the execution of constructor methods in languages such as Java. Accessing methods, however, can be identified only if the developers adhere to a particular naming scheme, such as through `put-` and `get-` prefixes in the method names. In contrast, a language such as C# again facilitates the identification of such accessor method join points because they are part of the language structure through the C# 'properties' language feature. In essence, we can say that the more structure is available in the implementation, the more properties are available for the definition of pointcuts, effectively facilitating their definition. However, structure that originates from programming conventions rather than language structure is usually not explicitly tied to a property that is available for use in a pointcut definition. This is especially problematic in languages with very few structural elements such as Smalltalk. In such languages, application development typically relies heavily on the use of programming conventions for the implementation of particular concepts such as accessors, constructors and many more application-specific concepts. As a result, aspect developers are forced to explicitly encode these conventions in pointcut expressions, often resulting in complex, fragile, and hard to maintain pointcut expressions.

The aspect-oriented programming language that is presented in this paper features an *open, logic-based* pointcut mechanism that allows to tie structural implementation conventions to explicit properties available for use in pointcut definitions. Our approach builds upon previous work on logic-based pointcut languages where we have described how the essential language features of a logic language render it into an adequate pointcut definition language [7]. In this paper, we further exploit the full power of the logic programming language for the definition of application-specific properties. In particular, we present an integration of the AspectS [8] and CARMA [9] aspect languages for Smalltalk. The result is an aspect-oriented programming language in which pointcuts can be defined in terms of an application-specific model that is asserted over the program. The application-specific model captures the structural conventions that are adhered to by the developers of the program and reifies them as explicit properties available for use in pointcut expressions. The model as well as the pointcuts are implemented using logic metaprograms in SOUL [10].

In the following section, we present AspectSOUL, the integration of the AspectS and CARMA aspect languages. Next, in section 3, we implement a number of pointcuts that rely on typical structural conventions that are adhered to by application developers in a Smalltalk environment. We explain how such pointcuts are complex, fragile, and hard to maintain and, in section 4, we describe how our AspectSOUL allows to tackle these issues through the definition of application-specific pointcuts, expressed in terms of an application-specific model. Section 5 applies the approach to aspects that operate on the drag and drop infrastructure of the UI framework and the refactoring browser in the Smalltalk environment. We summarize related and future work in section 6 before concluding the paper.

2 AspectSOUL

AspectSOUL is an integration of the CARMA pointcut language [9] and AspectS [8], a Smalltalk extension for aspect-oriented programming. Unlike most other approaches to aspect-oriented programming, AspectS does not extend the Smalltalk programming language with new language constructs for writing down aspects and advice expressions. Instead, AspectS is a framework approach to AOP. Pointcuts are written as Smalltalk expressions that return a collection of joinpoint descriptors. CARMA on the other hand, is a dedicated pointcut language based on logic programming. Naturally, such a dedicated query language offers advantages for writing pointcuts, as pointcuts are essentially queries over a joinpoint database. The integration of this logic-based pointcut language with AspectS further enforces the framework nature of AspectS by providing a full-fledged query-based pointcut language that can be extended with application-specific pointcut predicates. In essence, we combine the advantages of an extensible framework for defining advice expressions with the advantages of a dedicated and extensible pointcut language. In the remainder of this section, we introduce AspectS, CARMA, and their integration called AspectSOUL. In subsequent sections, we focus on how the open, logic-based pointcut language provides developers with an adequate means to handle complex and hard-to-maintain pointcut expressions.

2.1   AspectS

In the AspectS framework, aspects are implemented as subclasses of the class `AsAspect`. Its advices can be implemented as methods whose name begins with `advice` and which return an instance of `AsAdvice`. Two of the subclasses of `AsAdvice` can be used to implement either an around advice or a before/after advice. An instance can be created by calling a method which takes as its arguments qualifiers, a block implementing the pointcut, and blocks to implement the before, after or around effects of the advice.

An example advice method is shown in Figure 1. It specifies that any invocation of an `eventDoubleClick:` method implemented by `WindowSensor` or any of its subclasses should be logged. The effect of the advice is implemented in the block passed to the `beforeBlock:` parameter. When one of the methods specified by the pointcut needs to be executed, this block is executed right before the execution of the method's body. The block is passed a few arguments: the receiver object in which the method is executed, the arguments passed to the method, the aspect and the client. In this example, the block simply logs some of its arguments to the transcript. Note that it calls a method on `self`, aspect classes can implement regular methods besides advice methods as well. The pointcut is implemented by the block passed to the `pointcut:` argument. It returns a collection of `AsJoinpointDescriptor` instances. This collection is computed using the Smalltalk meta-object protocol and collection enumeration messages: the collection of `WindowSensor` and all of its subclasses is filtered to only those that implement a method named `eventDoubleClick:`, an `AsJoinpointDescriptor` is then collected for each of these.

Advice qualifiers specify dynamic conditions that should hold if the advice is to be executed. These conditions are implemented as activation blocks: blocks that take as arguments an aspect object and a stack frame. The framework defines a

```
adviceEventDoubleClick

^ AsBeforeAfterAdvice
    qualifier: (AsAdviceQualifier attributes: #(receiverInstanceSpecific))
    pointcut: [
      WindowSensor withAllSubclasses
        select: [:each |
          each includesSelector: #eventDoubleClick:]
        thenCollect: [:each |
          AsJoinPointDescriptor targetClass: each targetSelector: #eventDoubleClick:]]
    beforeBlock: [:receiver :arguments :aspect :client |
      self showHeader: '>>> EventDoubleClick >>>'
          receiver: receiver
          event: arguments first]
```

Fig. 1. Example advice definition in AspectS

number of activation blocks, that fall in two categories: checks done on the top of the stack, or on lower levels of the stack. The former are used for example to restrict advice execution to sender/receiver-specific activation: an advice on a method is only executed if the method is executed in a specific receiver object, or was invoked by a specific sender object, or is associated with a specific thread of control. The latter are used for control-flow related restrictions, such as only executing an advice on a method if the same method is not currently on the stack. The activation blocks have names, which are specified in the attributes of an `AsAdviceQualifier`. In the example advice, one activator block is specified: `receiverInstanceSpecific`.

Aspects can be woven into the Smalltalk image by sending an explicit `install` message to an aspect instance. The `install` method collects all advice objects in the class and executes their pointcut blocks to get the collection of joinpoint descriptors. The methods designated by these descriptors are then decorated by wrappers [11], one for each advice affecting this particular method. The wrappers check the activation blocks specified in their advice, passing them the aspect and the top stack frame (accessed using the `thisContext` reflective feature of Smalltalk [12]). If an activation condition does not hold, the wrapper simply executes the next wrapper (if any), or the original method. If all activation conditions hold, the wrapper executes the advice's around, before, and/or after block, and then proceeds to the next wrapper (if any) in the proper order, or the original method.

2.2 CARMA

CARMA is a pointcut language based on logic meta programming for reasoning about dynamic joinpoints. Unlike pointcuts in AspectS, CARMA pointcuts do not express conditions on methods, its joinpoints are representations of dynamic events in the execution of a Smalltalk program. CARMA defines a number of logic predicates for expressing conditions on these joinpoints, and pointcuts are written as logic queries using these predicates. It is possible to express conditions on dynamic values associated with the joinpoints. Furthermore, logic predicates are provided for querying the static structure of the Smalltalk program. These predicates are taken from the LiCoR library of logic predicates for logic meta programming [13]. The underlying language of this library and CARMA is the SOUL logic language [13,10].

The SOUL logic language is akin to Prolog [14], but has a few differences. Some of these are just syntactical, such as that variables are notated with question marks rather than capital letters, the ":-" symbol is written as `if`, and lists are written between angular (`<>`) instead of square brackets (`[]`). More importantly, SOUL is in linguistic symbiosis with the underlying Smalltalk language, allowing Smalltalk objects to be bound to logic variables and the execution of Smalltalk expressions as part of the logic program [15]. The symbiosis mechanism is what allows CARMA to express conditions on dynamic values associated with joinpoints which are actual Smalltalk objects, such as the arguments of a message.

The advantage of building a pointcut language on the logic programming paradigm lies in the declarative nature of this paradigm. No explicit control structures for looping over a set of classes or methods are necessary in point-cuts, as this is hidden in the logic language [16]. A pointcut simply states the conditions that a joinpoint should meet in order to activate an advice, without specifying how those joinpoints are computed. This makes declarative pointcuts, given some basic knowledge of logic programming of course, easier to read. A logic language also provides some advanced features such as unification that make it easier to write advanced pointcuts. A full discussion is outside the scope of this paper, but a more comprehensive analysis was given in earlier work [9]. In the next sections, we will however show how some of these features – particularly the ability to write multiple rules for the same predicate – are useful for writing model-based pointcuts.

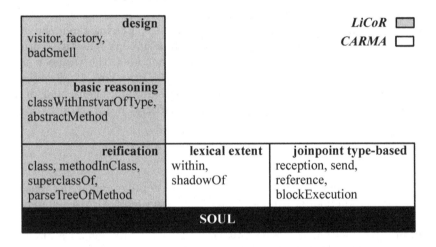

Fig. 2. Organization of, and example predicates in LiCoR and CARMA

The predicates in CARMA and LiCoR are organized into categories, as shown in Figure 2. The LiCoR predicates are organized hierarchically, with higher pred-icates defined in terms of the lower ones. The predicates in the "reification" cat-egory provide the fundamental access to the structure of a Smalltalk program: these predicates can be used to query the classes and methods in the program, and the fundamental relations between them such as which class is a superclass of which other class. The "basic reasoning" predicates define predicates that can be used to query more complex relations: which classes indirectly inherit from another class, which methods are abstract, which types an instance variable can possibly have etc. The "design" category contains predicates about design infor-mation in programs: there are for example predicates encoding design patterns [17] and refactoring "bad smells" [18].

The CARMA predicates access the dynamic structure of a Smalltalk program. There are two categories of predicates in CARMA, neither is defined in terms of each other, nor in terms of the LiCoR predicates. Nevertheless, the purpose of the "lexical extent" predicates is to link the dynamic and static structure, so that reasoning about both can be mixed in a pointcut. The `within` predicate for example can be used to express that a joinpoint is the result of executing an expression in a certain method. The "type-based" joinpoint predicates are the basic predicates of CARMA, they express conditions on certain types of joinpoints and basic data associated with those. An example is the `reception` predicate which is used to express that a joinpoint should be of the type "message reception", which means it represents the execution of a message to an object. Besides the joinpoint, the predicate has parameters for the basic associated data: the selector of the message and its arguments. There are also a few other predicates in CARMA (not shown in the figure), such as the `inObject` predicate which links a joinpoint to the object in which it is executed. In the case of a reception joinpoint, this is the receiver of the message.

A pointcut in CARMA is written as a logic query that results in joinpoints. By convention, the variable to which these are bound is called "`?jp`". The joinpoint representations should only be manipulated through the predicates provided by CARMA. An example pointcut is given in the next section.

2.3   CARMA Pointcuts in AspectS

AspectSOUL, the integration of CARMA with AspectS, is realized by subclassing the advice classes of AspectS so that a CARMA pointcut can be specified instead of a Smalltalk expression. The signature of the instance creation message for these subclasses is similar to the original. It takes as arguments a string with a CARMA pointcut, qualifiers and an around or before and/or after block. The message does a mapping to the instance creation message of the superclass. This is not a direct 1-on-1 mapping however, because CARMA pointcuts are about dynamic joinpoints, in contrast with the more static joinpoints of AspectS. Also, because AspectS does not support aspects that intercept block execution nor variable accesses or assignments, these features of CARMA are not adopted in AspectSOUL.

An example of an AspectS advice with a CARMA pointcut is shown in Figure 3. This is an around variant of the first example advice, with a pointcut that has the same effect. The first condition in the pointcut specifies that `?jp` must be a message reception joinpoint, where the selector of the message is `eventDoubleClick:`. The arguments of the message are bound to the variable `?args`. However, `?args` is not used any further in the pointcut which expresses that no conditions are put on the argument list. The second condition expresses that the joinpoint must occur lexically in a method with name `?selector` in the class `?class`. For a message reception joinpoint, this is effectively the method that is executed to handle the message. The final condition expresses that the class `?class` should be in the hierarchy of the class `WindowSensor`. The block has the same effect as in the first example, except that here it explicitly calls the next wrapper (if any) or original method.

```
adviceEventDoubleClick

^ AsCARMAAroundAdvice
    qualifier: (AsAdviceQualifier attributes: #())
    pointcutQuery: 'reception(?jp, #eventDoubleClick:, ?args),
                    within(?jp, ?class, ?selector),
                    classInHierarchyOf(?class, [WindowSensor])'
    aroundBlock: [:receiver :arguments :aspect :client :clientMethod |
      self showHeader: '>>> EventDoubleClick >>>'
          receiver: receiver
          event: arguments first.
      clientMethod valueWithReceiver: receiver arguments: arguments]
```

Fig. 3. Example AspectS advice definition with a CARMA pointcut

```
reception(?jp, #eventDoubleClick:, <?event>),
objectTestHolds(?event, #isYellow)
```

Fig. 4. A CARMA pointcut with a condition on a dynamic value

Figure 4 gives an example of a CARMA pointcut which does express conditions on the arguments of a message reception. The first condition expresses that ?jp must be a message reception joinpoint of the message eventDoubleClick:, where the argument list unifies with the list <?event>. Thus the argument list has to have one argument, which is bound to the variable ?event. The value of ?event is the actual Smalltalk event object that is sent as the argument of eventDoubleClick. The second condition uses the objectTestHolds predicate, which uses the symbiosis mechanism of SOUL to express that the object in ?event must respond true to the message isYellow. Thus, this pointcut captures joinpoints when a message about a double click event of the yellow mouse button is sent to some object. Expressing the same in AspectS can only be done by defining an appropriate qualifier, or by including the dynamic condition in the around block of the advice. The CARMA approach means that what conceptually should go into a pointcut can be better separated from the effect of the advice: that we only want to intercept double click events of the yellow mouse button is part of the "when" of the advice, not of the "what effect" it has. All of the qualifiers of AspectS can be expressed in CARMA, except for the control-flow qualifiers because CARMA does not currently support a construct similar to the cflow pointcut of AspectJ [19].

Two-phased weaving: The mapping done in the AspectSOUL advice subclasses to the original advice classes of AspectS involves the two-phase weaving model of CARMA. Because CARMA allows dynamic conditions and it is a Turing-complete language, it requires some advanced techniques to optimize weaving [9]. The mapping uses abstract interpretation [20] of the pointcuts to determine the methods which *may* lead to joinpoints matching the pointcut. For the pointcut of Figure 4, it determines that only executions of methods named eventDoubleClick: may match the pointcut. For these methods, AsJoinpointDescriptors are generated and passed to the advice superclass. The effect block passed to the superclass is wrapped so that it at run-time executes the pointcut to check if the joinpoint actually matches it, only then does it execute the effect of the advice. As such, the mapping splits the static and dynamic parts of the pointcut as one would normally do in AspectS by specifying dynamic conditions as part of the advice's effect block. Currently, the pointcut is fully re-executed at run-time, including the static conditions, except if it doesn't include any dynamic conditions. The use of more advanced partial evaluation [20] to further optimize weaving has been demonstrated [21], but a full discussion of two-phase weaving and the use of partial evaluation is beyond the scope of this paper.

In the following sections, we discuss how pointcut definitions easily become rather complex to implement and maintain, and how AspectSOUL provides developers with a means to manage this complexity.

3   Pointcuts Based on Structural Conventions

In the development of an application, developers often agree on particular programming conventions, design rules and patterns to structure their implementation. The intention of these structural implementation conventions is to render particular concepts more explicit in the implementation. For example, if all developers adhere to the same naming convention for all 'accessor' methods, we can more easily distinguish such accessors from any other method. More importantly, the implementation structure that is introduced by these conventions is also often exploited in pointcut definitions. In this section, we demonstrate this principle by studying the structural convention used to implement accessor and mutator methods, a simple but often-used pattern in Smalltalk. Next, we take a look at a couple of pointcuts which rely on these conventions to capture the execution of accessor methods. We demonstrate how, by implicitly capturing the notion of an accessor method using the coding conventions, the pointcut becomes more complex and easily suffers from the fragile pointcut problem.

3.1   Accessors and Mutators

In Smalltalk, clients are not allowed to directly access the instance variables of an object, and therefore they need to access them by means of dedicated methods. For each instance variable, a developer specifies an *accessor* method to retrieve the value of the variable, and a *mutator* method to change its value. Although these are regular Smalltalk methods, accessors and mutators are easily recognized since they are almost always implemented in an idiomatic way.

Most accessor and mutator methods are implemented according to the following structural convention:

- Both methods are classified in the **accessing** protocol;
- The selector of the *accessor* method corresponds with the name of the instance variable;
- The selector of the *mutator* method also corresponds with the name of the variable, however, this method takes one input parameter, namely the value to be assigned to the variable.

Moreover, the body of the accessor and mutator methods also follows a prototypical implementation. For example, suppose we have a **Person** class with an instance variable named **name**. The *accessor* and *mutator* methods for this variable are:

```
Person>>name
   ^name

Person>>name: anObject
   name := anObject
```

Since the join point models of current-day aspect languages do not explicitly reify these accessor and mutator methods as a separate kind of join points, aspect developers must exploit the structural conventions described above in order to capture the concept in a pointcut. For example, to capture all calls to accessor methods, the aspect developer can implement the following pointcut in AspectSOUL:

```
1   class(?class),
2   methodWithNameInClass(?method,?accessor,?class),
3   instanceVariableInClassChain(?accessor,?class),
4   methodInProtocol(?method, accessing),
5   reception(?joinpoint,?accessor,?args),
6   withinClass(?joinpoint,?class)
```

The above pointcut makes the implicit assumption that accessor methods are rigorously implemented using the naming scheme in which the name of the method corresponds with the name of the instance variable. Lines 1 to 4 of the pointcut reflect the naming convention on which the pointcut is based. These lines select all messages corresponding to the name of an instance variable, and whose method is also classified in the **accessing** protocol. Lines 5 and 6 will intercept all messages which correspond to the naming convention.

As long as the developers of the base code adhere to the naming convention on which the pointcut relies, it will correctly capture all accessors. However, if a developer of the base program deviates from the naming convention, by for instance renaming the instance variable without also renaming the selector of the accessor, the pointcut no longer captures the correct set of join points. Instead of relying on naming conventions, a pointcut developer can also exploit the stereotypical implementation of accessor methods. This would result in the following pointcut:

```
1   class(?class),
2   methodWithNameInClass(?method,?selector,?class),
3   instanceVariableInClassChain(?var,?class),
4   returnStatement(?method,variable(?var)),
5   reception(?joinpoint,?selector,?args),
6   withinClass(?joinpoint,?class)
```

Lines 1 – 4 of the pointcut above select all methods which contain a return statement that directly returns the value of an instance variable. As with the previous pointcut, lines 5 and 6 capture all occurrences of these methods. While this pointcut is not fragile with respect to changes in the names of instance variables, it still assumes that the base code developer rigorously followed the implementation idiom. However, often there exist slight variations on the programming idioms on which a pointcut is based. Consider for instance the following accessor method:

```
Person>>friends
   ^ friends isNil ifTrue:[friends := OrderedCollection new] ifFalse:[friends].
```

This method presents a variation on the often-used programming idiom for accessor methods. Instead of directly returning the value of the instance variable, the method checks wether the variable has already been initialized, and if not, will set its value to an empty `OrderedCollection`. It is clear that this lazy-initialised version of accessor methods will not be captured by the pointcut which assumes that the accessor is implemented using a return statement that directly returns the value of the variable. In other words, the pattern that is expressed in the previous pointcut does not apply to this method, although it is an accessor method.

3.2 Complexity and Fragility

Although the example pointcuts described above rely on a rather simple structural implementation convention, their definition and maintenance is already a rather complex activity. First of all, an aspect developer needs to know and understand the intricate implementation details of the structural convention and implement a pointcut expression for it. The lazy-initialized accessor methods in the example above illustrate that there often exist a number of variations to the programming conventions used to implement a certain concept. Therefore, any pointcut that needs to capture the execution of an accessor method needs to capture all possible variations, which easily leads to complex and lengthy pointcut expressions. This is especially the case because the part of the pointcut which reasons about the join points and the part which expresses the structural convention are not clearly separated. In our example above, the first four lines of both pointcuts express the coding convention, while the last two lines perform the actual selection of join points which are associated with the accessor methods. It is not instantly clear which part of the pointcut reflects the coding convention, further complicating the reuse and maintenance of the pointcut expression.

Finally, the aspect developer must also carefully analyse the changes and additions to the base program in subsequent evolutions, which are possibly made by other developers. In essence, the definition of a pointcut that explicitly relies on structural conventions to capture an application-specific concept easily suffers from the fragile pointcut problem [22]. Due to the tight coupling between the pointcut and the implementation, seemingly safe modifications to the implementation may result in the pointcut no longer capturing the correct set of join points. For example, if the base program developers do not adhere to the coding conventions, or change the convention by for instance using the prefixes put- and get- to indicate a mutator or an accessor method respectively, the pointcut no longer captures the correct set of join points.

4 Application-Specific Pointcuts and Models

We alleviate the problems associated with low-level pointcut definitions through the definition of *application-specific pointcuts* that are expressed in terms of an *application-specific* model. Such an application-specific model is implemented as an extension to the pointcut mechanism and it identifies high-level, application-specific properties in the implementation and makes them available for use in pointcuts. Aspect developers can make use of these properties to define application-specific pointcuts, i.e. pointcuts that are no longer defined in terms of the low-level implementation details but, instead, are defined in terms of application-specific properties defined by the model. As a result, the intricate low-level details in the implementation remain confined to the implementation of the application-specific model, which is also the responsibility of the base program developers. The application-specific model effectively becomes an additional abstraction layer that is imposed over the implementation and it acts as a contract between the base program developers and the aspect developers.

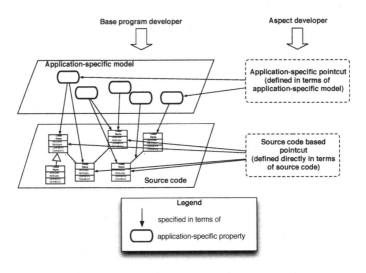

Fig. 5. Application-specific pointcuts are defined in terms of an application-specific model

Figure 5 illustrates how application-specific pointcuts, implemented by the aspect developers, depend on the definition of the application-specific model that is certified by the base program developers. The application-specific pointcuts are defined in terms of the application-specific model which, in turn, is defined in terms of the implementation. This decoupling of the pointcuts from the intricate details of the implementation allows that base program developers define and maintain the application-specific model. In other words, the tight coupling to the implementation that is present in the source-code based pointcuts is effectively transferred to a more appropriate location, i.e. the definition of the application-specific model.

Both the application-specific pointcuts and the application-specific model are implemented using SOUL logic metaprograms. In essence, the application-specific model defines a set of logic predicates that reify application-specific properties of the implementation, based on the conventions that are adhered to by the developers. Because the application-specific model is built as an extension to the pointcut mechanism, aspect developers can straightforwardly use these predicates in the definition of application-specific pointcuts to access the application-specific properties. Furthermore, the essential features of a logic language also facilitate the use and extension of the application-specific model.

In the following subsection, we define application-specific models for the accessors convention that was described in the previous section. Subsequently, we use these models to redefine the pointcuts of the previous section into application-specific pointcuts.

4.1   Application-Specific Model

An application-specific model defines a set of logic predicates that are available for use in an (application-specific) pointcut. These logic predicates are implemented using SOUL logic metaprograms. We illustrate the definition of an application-specific model by means of the accessors and mutators example.

The model that defines the accessor and mutator method properties consists of two predicates:

```
accessor(?class,?method,?var)
mutator(?class,?method,?var)
```

These predicates declare the accessor and mutator properties over methods named ?method defined in ?class. Furthermore, they also extract the name of the variable ?var that is accessed or modified. The implementation of these predicates captures the coding convention that is followed by the developer of the application. For example, the accessor predicate is implemented as follows:

```
accessor(?class,?varName,?varName) if
    class(?class),
    instanceVariableInClassChain(?varName,?class),
    methodWithNameInClass(?method,?varName,?class),
    methodInProtocol(?method, accessing),
    accessorForm(?method,?varName).

accessorForm(?method,?var) if
    returnStatement(?method,variable(?var))
```

The logic program above consists of two rules that each implement a predicate: `accessor` and `accessorForm`. The first predicate is defined in terms of the second one and a variety of predicates that are available in LiCoR. The first rule captures the naming convention of accessor methods as well as their classification in the 'accessing' protocol, as we described earlier. The verification of the idiomatic implementation of the accessor method is located in the second rule. This rule verifies if the method's implementation consists of a single return statement that consists of a single expression: the variable. As a consequence, the above logic metaprogram classifies methods of the following form as accessor methods:

```
Person>>name
    ^name
```

4.2   Application-Specific Pointcuts

Once the application-specific model is defined by the base program developers, the aspect developers can use it to define application-specific pointcuts. For example, the application-specific pointcut that captures the execution of accessor methods can now be written as follows:

```
reception(?joinpoint,?selector,?args),
accessor(?class,?selector,?var)
```

This application-specific pointcut no longer relies on a particular coding convention for accessor methods, as opposed to source-code based pointcuts. Instead, it relies on the application-specific property of an accessor method that is provided by the application-specific model. The base program developers ensure that this model is maintained such that all accessor methods are correctly identified. Furthermore, because the pointcut definition now explicitly states that it captures the execution of accessor methods, it is more readable and understandable to other developers. Of course, the above pointcut is a rather simple use of a single application-specific property. However, a single application-specific property does not correspond to a single pointcut. For example, consider the following pointcut that is defined in terms of the accessor and mutator properties:

```
reception(?joinpoint,?selector,?args),
accessor(?class,?selector,?var),
mutator(?class,?otherSelector,?var)
```

This pointcut matches all accessor method execution join points for variables for which there also exists a mutator method. It can, for example, be used in a synchronisation aspect to execute a write lock advice.

4.3   Model Specialisation

A specific advantage of building the application-specific model using a logic metalanguage is that we can easily extend the model through the definition of alternative logic rules for existing predicates. For example, the application-specific model that we defined above does not classify all accessor methods correctly. There exist many more possible implementations of accessor methods, such as the lazy-initialisation presented in section 3.1. Because the coding convention is now explicitly defined in the application-specific model and because the application-specific model is restricted to the coding conventions only, the base program developers can easily extend it to accommodate additional accessor forms. This is in contrast to when the coding convention is implicitly used in a pointcut definition. More importantly, because the model is defined as a logic metaprogram, additional accessor forms can be defined using alternative definitions for the accessor predicate. For example, we can extend the definition of this property to include lazy-initialised accessor methods by including the following logic rule:

```
accessorForm(?method,?var) if
    returnStatement(?method,send(?nilCheck,[#'ifTrue:ifFalse:' ],<?trueBlock,?falseBlock>)),
    nilCheckStatement(?nilCheck,?var),
    statementsOfBlock(<assign(?var,?varinit)>,?trueBlock),
    statementsOfBlock(<?var>,?falseBlock)
```

The above logic metaprogram provides an alternative definition for the
`accessorForm` predicate. These alternatives are placed in a logical disjunction
and, as a result, our application-specific model also ties the accessor property to
methods of the following form:

```
Person>>friends
    ^ friends isNil ifTrue:[friends := OrderedCollection new] ifFalse:[friends].
```

However, the following accessor method does not correspond to the coding
convention:

```
Person>>phoneNumbers
    ^ phoneNumbers ifNil:[phoneNumbers := OrderedCollection new] ifNotNil:[phoneNumbers].
```

Therefore, we can again define an alternative logic rule that detects accessor
methods of the above form:

```
accessorForm(?method,?var) if
    returnStatement(?method,send(?var,[#'ifNil:ifNotNil:' ],<?nilBlock,?notNilBlock>)),
    statementsOfBlock(<assign(?var,?varinit)>,?nilBlock),
    statementsOfBlock(<?var>,?notNilBlock)
```

Such a model specialisation is particularly useful if different developers implement different modules of the same base program. If all developers agree on
a single application-specific model (i.e. a set of properties implemented by predicates), they can each follow their own programming convention to implement
each property. For example, one set of developers might even agree on the use
of **put** and **get** prefixes for all accessor methods while other developers can follow the common Smalltalk convention that we just explained. The first group of
developers then needs to define an alternative logic rule that correctly detects
methods prefixed with **put** and **get** and implemented in their part of the base
program as accessor methods.

4.4   Property Parameters and Unification

The definition of an application-specific model using a logic metalanguage does
not only allow developers to associate structural conventions to properties available for use in pointcuts. In addition, the properties can be parameterized *and*
expose values associated to the property. For example, the accessor predicate
does not only expose particular methods as accessor methods, it also exposes
the actual variable that is accessed by the method[1]. More precisely, because a
logic language does not make a distinction between arguments and return values,
the variable that is accessed is also automatically a parameter of the accessor
predicate. This also holds for all other parameters of the accessor predicate: they
can act both as parameters as well as return values associated to the property.
In essence, the logic language feature of 'unification' allows that we can automatically use the application-specific property that is defined by the accessor
predicate in multiple ways, i.e. any argument of the predicate can be bound or
unbound. A couple of examples are illustrated in the following code excerpt.
Each line represents a separate use of the **accessor** predicate.

---

[1] Mind that the method name can be different from the variable name, depending on
the actual coding convention.

```
1    accessor(?class,?selector,?var)
2    accessor([Array],#at:put:,?var)
3    accessor(?class,?selector,#name)
```

The first line will retrieve all accessor methods and expose their class, method-name and accessed variable. The second line checks if the `at:put:` method in the `Array` class is an accessor method and retrieves its accessed variable. Finally, the use of the `accessor` predicate on the last line retrieves all accessor methods that access a variable named `name`.

5   Application-Specific Models in Practice

The accessors and mutators example is a valuable application-specific model but relies on very simple coding conventions. In the development of a Smalltalk application, there are many more conventions that can be used to expose application-specific properties valuable for use in a pointcut definition. We illustrate the use of two such conventions in the following subsections. In particular, we build a model that exposes properties based on structural conventions used in the *drag and drop framework* of the user-interface and the *implementation of refactorings* in the refactoring browser in Visualworks Smalltalk.

5.1   Drag and Drop Application-Specific Model

The drag and drop facilities in VisualWorks Smalltalk are implemented by means of a lightweight framework. This framework identifies a number of hooks that allow a developer to implement the drag and drop behaviour for his particular application. These hooks are:

- **Drag Ok:** a predicate to check wether the current widget may initiate a drag;
- **Start Drag:** actions which need to take place in order to start the drag (e.g. creating a drag and drop context, . . .);
- **Enter Drag/Exit Drag:** these hooks are triggered whenever during a drag, the mouse pointer enters/exists the boundaries of a certain widget;
- **Over Drag:** actions which are executed when the pointer is hovering over a widget during a drag (e.g. change the cursor);
- **Drop:** actions which take place when an element is dropped on a widget.

A developer can add drag and drop functionality to an application by associating methods with the hooks specified above. This is done by means of the `windowSpec` system of the VisualWorks user interface framework. A `windowSpec` is a declarative specification of the different widgets which make up the user interface of an application. This specification is then used by the user interface framework to construct the actual interface. In the `windowSpec`, the developer can, for each widget, associate methods with the different hooks of the drag and drop framework. In order to access the data which is being dragged, the origin of the drag operation, etc. these methods pass around a `DragDropManager` object.

The structure of the framework described above can be used to define an application-specific model that associates methods to an explicit drag and drop property: i.e. for each of the hooks defined above, we define a separate predicate. For example, we define the `dragEnterMethod(?class,?sel,?comp)` predicate that classifies all methods that implement the 'drag enter' hook. Furthermore, this predicate exposes the name of the visual component in the interface that is dragged over. This predicate allows aspect developers to write application-specific pointcuts that capture a drag event as the execution of such a method:

```
reception(?jp,?selector,?args),
dragEnterMethod(?class,?selector,?component)
```

Furthermore, we also define the `draggedObject(?dragdropmanager,?object)` and `dragSource(?dragdropmanager,?source)` predicates that reify the object being dragged and the source component from where it is being dragged respectively. Both predicates extract this information from the `DragDropManager` instance that is being passed as an argument to the drag and drop methods. We can now further extend the pointcut such that it only captures drag events that originate from a particular source or drags of a particular object. For example, we complete the above pointcut with the following conditions to capture drags originating from a `FigureManager` (lines 2–3) and dragging a `Line` object (lines 4–5). The first line merely extracts the only argument being passed to the 'drag enter' method, which is the `DragDropManager` object.

```
1    equals(?args,<?dragdropmanager>),
2    dragSource(?dragdropmanager,?source),
3    instanceOf(?source,[FigureManager]),
4    draggedObject(?dragdropmanager,?object),
5    instanceOf(?object,Line)
```

This pointcut is particularly useful for the definition of an aspect that renders an icon in our user-interface depending on the element that is being dragged. Without aspects, we would need to implement the visualisation of such an icon in the 'drag enter' method of every application model in our user-interface, resulting in duplicated and scattered code. Furthermore, the application-specific model now also allows us to decouple the pointcut definition from the actual structural conventions used in the user-interface framework and implement them in terms of the explicit application-specific properties associated to a user-interface.

5.2   Refactorings

Refactorings are behaviour-preserving program transformations which can be used to improve the structure of the application [18]. A number of these refactorings can be automated up to a certain degree, which has resulted in the development of tool support for performing refactorings directly from the IDE. In VisualWorks, such tool support is integrated with the `Refactoring Browser`.

The `Refactoring Browser` makes use of a framework implementing these refactorings. In this framework, all refactorings are represented by a subclass of the abstract `Refactoring` class. Each subclass must implement a `preconditions` method, which specifies the preconditions that the source code to be refactored needs to adhere to in order to perform the refactoring, and a **transform** method, which performs the actual program transformation.

As an example of an aspect based on the refactoring framework, consider a software engineering tool (for instance a versioning system) which, each time a refactoring is initiated, needs to be notified of the program entities which are possibly affected by the refactoring. Such information is hard to retrieve from the source code of the framework. However, by creating an application-specific model for the refactoring framework, we can explicitly document this additional information. The following pointcut retrieves all affected entities for the instantiation of a refactoring:

```
reception(?joinpoint,?message,?arguments),
inObject(?joinpoint,?receiver),
refactoringInstantiation(?receiver,?message,?arguments,?affectedentities)
```

The first two lines of the pointcut select all message receptions and their receiver; the last line restricts these message receptions to the ones which instantiate a refactoring. Also, the pointcut binds all affected entities, depending on the input and the type of the refactoring to the variable ?affectedentities.

The refactoringInstantiation rule is defined as follows:

```
1    refactoringInstantiation(?refactoring,?message,?args,?affectedentity) if
2      refactoring(?refactoring),
3      methodWithNameInClass(?method,?message,?refactoring),
4      instanceCreationMethod(?method),
5      refactoringAffectedEntity(?refactoring,?refactoringclass,?args,?affectedentity)
```

The first line of this rule checks wether the receiver of the message is a refactoring (i.e. wether it is a subclass of the class **Refactoring**). The second and third line implement the selection of those messages (and their arguments) which create an instance of the refactoring. Finally, the last line calculates, based on the arguments of the message, the program entities which can be affected by the refactoring.

For each refactoring, the affected entities are explicitly documented by logic rules.

```
refactoringAffectedEntity(?refactoring,[PushUpMethodRefactoring],?input,?affectedentity) if
  originalClassOfPushUpMethod(?input,?affectedentity)

refactoringAffectedEntity(?refactoring,[PushUpMethodRefactoring],?input,?affectedentity) if
  originalClassOfPushUpMethod(?input,?class),
  superclassOf(?affectedentity,?class).
```

The above rules reflect this knowledge for the **Method Push Up**-refactoring. The first line of both rules extracts the class of the method which will be pushed up from the arguments of the message reception. For this refactoring, both the class from which the refactoring is initiated (the first rule), as well as its superclass are affected (the second rule).

6   Related and Future Work

In previous work [23], we have introduced the technique of *model-based pointcuts* that allows to define pointcuts in a similar way as the application-specific pointcuts presented in this paper. In fact, the approach presented in this paper is a first step towards an improved integration of model-based pointcuts and logic-based pointcut languages [7]. In essence, we further extended the technique of model-based pointcuts to exploit the full power of the logic programming language for the definition of application-specific properties. In [23], we merely extended the pointcut language with a single predicate that allows to query a conceptual model of the program, implemented using intensional views [24]. In this paper, the model consists of full logic predicates, resulting in an improved integration of the model and the pointcuts. In contrast, in [23], we have shown how model-based pointcuts are less fragile with respect to changes in the base program primarily due to tool support that enforces developers to adhere to the correct conventions such that the model remains valid. In this paper, we have focused on the adequate features of a logic language for the creation and extension of the model and we presented an improved integration of the model with the pointcut mechanism itself. We are currently working on how to reconcile the support for the detection of the fragile pointcut problem with the full power of the application-specific models presented in this paper. Furthermore, there are a number of related approaches or techniques that work towards the same goal:

6.1 Expressive Pointcut Languages

Some recent experimental aspect-oriented languages also propose more advanced pointcut languages. The Alpha aspect language, for example, also uses a logic programming language for the specification of pointcuts and enhances the expressiveness by providing diverse automatically-derived models of the program. These models and their associated predicates can, for example, reason over the entire state and execution history [25]. In particular, Ostermann and Mezini have also identified how to build user-defined pointcut predicates using a logic language. EAOP [26] and JAsCo [27] offer event-based or stateful pointcuts that allow to express the activation of an aspect based on a sequence of events during the program's execution.

6.2 Annotations

An alternative approach to application-specific pointcuts over application-specific models is to define pointcuts in terms of explicit annotations in the code [28,29]. Annotations classify source-code entities and thereby make explicit additional semantics that would otherwise be expressed through implicit programming conventions. This approach, however, does not benefit from the expressive power that is provided by the logic metalanguage.

6.3 Design Rules and XPI

Yet another alternative approach is to explicitly include the pointcut descriptions in the design and implementation of the software and to require developers to adhere to this design. Sullivan et al. [30] propose such an approach by interfacing base code and aspect code through *design rules*. These rules are documented in interface specifications that base code designers are constrained to 'implement', and that aspect designers are licensed to depend upon. Once the interfaces are defined (and respected), aspect and base code become symmetrically oblivious to each others' design decisions. More recently, the interfaces that are defined by the design rules can be implemented as *Explicit Pointcut Interfaces* (XPI's) using AspectJ [31]. Using XPIs, pointcuts are declared globally and some constraints can be verified on these pointcuts using other pointcuts. Our approach is different in the fact that we keep the pointcut description in the aspect, leaving more flexibility to the aspect developer. While XPIs fix all pointcut interfaces beforehand, our application-specific model only fixes the specific properties available for use in pointcut definitions.

7 Conclusion

AspectSOUL is an extension of the AspectS language framework with the open-ended logic-based pointcut language of CARMA. The resulting integrated aspect language allows developers to extend the pointcut language with an application-specific model. Such an application-specific model defines new pointcut predicates that reify implicit structural implementation conventions as explicit properties available for use in pointcut definitions. These *model-based pointcuts* are decoupled from the intricate structural implementation details of the base program, effectively reducing their complexity. The definition of the application-specific model confines all these technical details and serves as a contract between the base program developers and the aspect developers. Finally, the logic paradigm offers adequate language features for the definition and extension of the application-specific model.

References

1. Kiczales, G., Lamping, J., Mendhekar, A., Maeda, C., Lopes, C.V., Loingtier, J.M., Irwin, J.: Aspect-oriented programming. In: Proceedings of the European Conference on Object-Oriented Programming (ECOOP). Number 1241 in LNCS, Springer-Verlag (June 1997)
2. Filman, R.E., Elrad, T., Clarke, S., Aksit, M.: Aspect-Oriented Software Development. Addison-Wesley (2004)
3. Kiczales, G., Lamping, J., Mendhekar, A., Maeda, C., Lopes, C., Loingtoir, J., Irwin, J.: Aspect-oriented programming. In: European Conference on Object-Oriented Programming (ECOOP). LNCS, Springer Verlag (1997) 220–242
4. Parnas, D.L.: On the criteria to be used in decomposing systems into modules. Communications of the ACM **15**(12) (December 1972) 1053–1058
5. Xu, J., Rajan, H., Sullivan, K.: Understanding aspects via implicit invocation. In: Automated Software Engineering (ASE), IEEE Computer Society Press (2004)
6. Filman, R., Friedman, D.: Aspect-oriented programming is quantification and obliviousness (2000) Workshop on Advanced Separation of Concerns (OOPSLA).
7. Gybels, K., Brichau, J.: Arranging language features for more robust pattern-based crosscuts. In: Aspect-Oriented Software Development (AOSD). (2003)

8. Hirschfeld, R.: Aspect-Oriented Programming with Aspects. In: Lecture Notes in Computer Science: Objects, Components, Architectures, Services, and Applications for a NetworkedWorld: International Conference NetObjectDays, NODe 2002, Erfurt, Germany, October 7–10, 2002. Revised Papers. (2003)

9. Gybels, K., Brichau, J.: Arranging language features for more robust pattern-based crosscuts. In: Proceedings of the Second International Conference of Aspect-Oriented Software Development. (2003)

10. : The Smalltalk Open Unification Language (SOUL). http://prog.vub.ac.be/SOUL

11. Brant, J., Foote, B., Johnson, R.E., Roberts, D.: Wrappers to the rescue. Lecture Notes in Computer Science (1998)

12. Rivard, F.: Smalltalk: a reflective language. In: Proceedings of the Reflection Conference 1996. (1996)

13. Mens, K., Michiels, I., Wuyts, R.: Supporting software development through declaratively codified programming patterns. Journal on Expert Systems with Applications **23**(4) (2002) 405–413

14. Nilsson, U., M, J.: Logic, Programming and Prolog. Second edition edn. John Wiley & Sons (1995)

15. Gybels, K., Wuyts, R., Ducasse, S., D'Hondt, M.: Inter-language reflection: A conceptual model and its implementation. Elsevier Journal on Computer Languages, Systems & Structures **32** (2006) 109 – 124

16. Kowalski, R.: Algorithm = logic + control. Communications of the ACM **22**(7) (1979) 424–436

17. Gamma, E., Helm, R., Johnson, R., Vlissides, J.: Design Patterns, Elements of Reusable Object-Oriented Software. Addison-Wesley (1995)

18. Fowler, M.: Refactoring: Improving the Design of Existing Code. Addison-Wesley (1999)

19. Lopes, C., Hilsdale, E., Hugunin, J., Kersten, M., Kiczales, G.: Illustrations of crosscutting. In Tarr, P., D'Hondt, M., Lopes, C., Bergmans, L., eds.: International Workshop on Aspects and Dimensional Computing at ECOOP. (2000)

20. Jones, N.D., Gomard, C.K., Sestoft, P.: Partial Evaluation and Automatic Program Generation. Prentice Hall International (1993)

21. Masuhara, H., Kiczales, G., Dutchyn, C.: Compilation semantics of aspect-oriented programs. In Leavens, G.T., Cytron, R., eds.: Foundations of Aspect-Oriented Languages Workshop at AOSD 2002. Number 02-06 in Tech Report, Department of Computer Science, Iowa State University (2002) 17–26

22. Koppen, C., Stoerzer, M.: Pcdiff: Attacking the fragile pointcut problem. In: First European Interactive Workshop on Aspects in Software (EIWAS). (2004)

23. Kellens, A., Mens, K., Brichau, J., Gybels, K.: Managing the evolution of aspect-oriented software with model-based pointcuts. In: In Proceedings of the European Conference on Object-Oriented Programming (ECOOP), Spring-Verlag (2006)

24. Mens, K., Kellens, A., Pluquet, F., Wuyts, R.: Co-evolving code and design with intensional views - a case study. Computer Languages, Systems and Structures **32**(2-3) (July-October 2006) 140–156

25. Ostermann, K., Mezini, M. Bockisch, C.: Expressive pointcuts for increased modularity. In: European Conference on Object-Oriented Programming (ECOOP). (2005)

26. Douence, R., Fritz, T., Loriant, N., Menaud, J.M., Ségura, M., Südholt, M.: An expressive aspect language for system applications with arachne. In: Aspect-Oriented Software Development (AOSD). (2005)

27. Vanderperren, W., Suvee, D., Cibran, M.A., De Fraine, B.: Stateful aspects in JAsCo. In: Software Composition (SC). LNCS (2005)

28. Havinga, W., Nagy, I., Bergmans, L.: Introduction and derivation of annotations in AOP: Applying expressive pointcut languages to introductions. In: First European Interactive Workshop on Aspects in Software. (2005)
29. Kiczales, G., Mezini, M.: Separation of concerns with procedures, annotations, advice and pointcuts. In: European Conference on Object-Oriented Programming (ECOOP). LNCS, Springer Verlag (2005)
30. Sullivan, K., Griswold, W., Song, Y., Chai, Y., Shonle, M., Tewari, N., Rajan, H.: On the criteria to be used in decomposing systems into aspects. In: Symposium on the Foundations of Software Engineering joint with the European Software Engineering Conference (ESEC/FSE 2005), ACM Press (2005)
31. Griswold, W., Sullivan, K., Song, Y., Shonle, M., Teware, N., Cai, Y., Rajan.H.: Modular software design with crosscutting interfaces. IEEE Software, Special Issue on Aspect-Oriented Programming (January/February 2006)

An Object-Oriented Approach for Context-Aware Applications*

Andrés Fortier[1,2], Nicolás Cañibano[1], Julián Grigera[1], Gustavo Rossi[1,3],
and Silvia Gordillo[1,4]

[1] LIFIA, Facultad de Informática, UNLP, La Plata, Argentina
[2] DSIC, Universidad Politécnica de Valencia, Valencia, España
[3] CONICET
[4] CICPBA
{andres,cani,juliang,gustavo,gordillo}@lifia.info.unlp.edu.ar

Abstract. In this paper we present a novel, object-oriented approach for designing and building applications that provide context-aware services. Our approach emphasizes a clear separation of the relevant concerns in the application (base behavior, context-sensitive properties, services, sensing technologies, etc.) to improve modularity and thus simplify evolution. We first motivate the problem with a simple scenario of a virtual campus; we next present a new context model, which emphasizes on behavior instead of data. We next show the main components of our architecture and a simple approach to achieve a clear separation of concerns. We analyze the most important (sub) models in which we decompose a context-aware application and explain the use of dependency mechanisms to achieve loosely coupled relationships between objects. We also show how to take advantage of a reflective environment like Smalltalk to adapt the application's behavior dynamically and to provide transparent object distribution. We finally compare our work with others and discuss some further work we are pursuing.

1 Introduction: The Challenges of Context-Awareness

Context-Aware (and in particular Location-Aware) applications are hard to build and more difficult to maintain due to their *organic* nature [1]. For this reason, improving modularity and reducing tightly-coupled relationships between objects is extremely necessary when designing this kind of software.

Among the many issues involved in developing and maintaining context-aware systems, we consider the following as the main difficulties:

- **Context-aware systems integrate knowledge from different areas** such as HCI, artificial intelligence, software engineering and context sensing to produce the final application. Due to the extent of this discipline, we consider that the next generation of context-aware systems will need an integrating platform rather than a single application [6].

---

* This paper has been partially supported by the SeCyT under the project PICT 13623.

W. De Meuter (Ed.): ISC 2006, LNCS 4406, pp. 23–46, 2007.
© Springer-Verlag Berlin Heidelberg 2007

- **Context information is acquired from non-traditional devices and distributed sources**, and must then be abstracted and interpreted to be used by applications [4].
- **Abstracting context means more than changing representation**. While interpreted context data is usually dealt as string data, applications are composed of objects, and many times those objects represent contextual information as well. There is a certain impedance mismatch between context and application data, even when they refer to the same concept.
- **Adapting to context is hard**; design issues related with context-aware adaptation are not completely understood and thus handled incorrectly. For example, the rule-based paradigm has been over-used in the last few years to express adaptation policies, such as: "When being in a room, provide services A, B and C". While rules can be often useful (especially when we want to give the user the control of building his own rules), we claim that more elaborated structures are necessary to improve maintenance and evolution.
- **Context-related information is usually "tangled" with other application data**; for example, the location of an application object (which is necessary to detect when the user is near the object) is coupled with others object's concerns, making evolution of both types of characteristics difficult.

Our research deals with the identification of recurrent problems and design micro-architectures in context-aware software. In this paper we describe an architectural approach for dealing with the problem of providing context-aware services. Our approach is based on a clear separation of concerns that allows us not only to decouple context sensing and acquisition (as in [14]), but mainly to improve separation of application modules, to ease extension and maintenance. For this purpose we make an extensive use of dependency mechanisms to provide context-aware services and take advantage of the reflective nature of the Smalltalk environment to dynamically change objects' behavior and achieve transparent distribution.

The main contributions of our paper are the following:

- We show how to separate application concerns related with context awareness to improve modularity. This approach can be used to build new applications or to extend legacy ones by adding location and other context-aware services. A concrete architecture that supports this approach is presented.
- We show how to objectify services and make them dependent of changes of context; in particular we emphasize location-aware services.
- We introduce a behavioral point of view to deal with contextual information (instead of the current data view of most existing approaches).
- We show how to use the reflective capabilities of Smalltalk to model our conception of context.
- We show how to take advantage of transparent distribution mechanisms in mobile environments.

2   Motivating Example

Suppose we are adapting an existing software system in a University Campus to provide context-based services (in particular location-based ones), in the style of the example in [16]. Our system already provides information about careers, courses, professors, timetables, etc. We now want users carrying their preferred devices to interact with the system while they move around the campus. For example, when a student enters a classroom, he can get the corresponding course's material, information about its professor, etc. At the same time, those services corresponding to the containing location context (the Campus) should be also available. When he moves to the sport area, the course's related services disappear and he receives information about upcoming sport events. Even though we use the user's location as an example, different contextual information such as the user's role or activity might also shape the software answer. For example, we could infer whether the student is attending to a lecture by sensing his position, checking his timetable, verifying the teacher's position and sensing the noise level in the classroom. As a consequence, the student's smarthpone could be switched to silent mode so that it doesn't interrupt the teacher in the middle of his lecture.

The first design problem we must face is how to seamlessly extend our application in order to make it location-aware, i.e. to provide services that correspond to the actual location context. The next challenge involves adapting the behavior to the user's role (a professor, student, etc) and other contextual parameters such as current time or activity. While applications of this kind have always been built almost completely from scratch, we consider that this will not be the case if context-aware computing becomes mainstream; we will have to adapt dozens of legacy applications by adding context-aware behavior.

When working with context-aware applications we can find typical evolution patterns such as adding new services related to a particular location, improving sensing mechanisms (for example moving from GPS to infrared), changing the location model (from symbolic to geometric [11]), and so on. While most technological requirements in this scenario can be fulfilled using state-of-the art hardware and communication devices, there are many design problems that need some further study:

- During the day the user is involved in a set of activities that constantly change what is contextually relevant. How do we model context so that it can follow this changes and effectively adapt to the user's needs?
- How can the system adapt to appearing (previously unknown) sensing devices? For example, in the moment the user enters in the range of a wi-fi access point new sensing devices may be available through the network. This new sensing information can be used to improve the user's context and therefore improve the system response to user's needs.
- Context information can be provided by a variety of sensing devices during a short period of time; for example, the weather conditions can be acquired from a software sensor (a web service when an Internet connection is available) or from a hardware device (a simple weather station installed in the

building accessed through a sensor network). Thus, even thought context is mainly built from sensing information, to easily adapt it to different technologies, it should be as loosely coupled as possible from the sensing mechanisms. How do we model this relationship?

– Context-aware behavior may depend on application functionality, but this kind of functionality tends to be volatile in comparison with the core application. How can the application cooperate with context-ware behavior in a way that changes in the later don't impact on the former?

The aim of this paper is to focus these problems, mainly those that characterize the difficulties for software evolution and to show how combining proven design principles with reflective facilities can yield a scalable architecture to build context-aware software.

3   Our Context Model

Even though context is recognized as having a dynamic nature, it is usually treated as a fixed piece of data upon which some behavior is executed, which we consider neglects its essence. From our point of view, context should be modeled as close as possible to the phenomenological view presented by Dourish [5]. Taking his definition as a starting point, we claim that the following properties must hold when modeling context:

1. *Context is not passive.* The context model must take an active role in the application and shouldn't be considered as a static collection of data. If decisions must be taken according to the context, then the context itself should be actively involved in that process.

2. *Context is not stable and can not be defined in advance.* Since context is inherently dynamic, we can not constraint the context information that will be modeled when designing the application. Since context-aware applications are supposed to adapt to the user's activities, what is contextually relevant to the user is constantly changing. Therefore, our model of context should be able to represent these dynamically varying aspects of the user's context that are relevant in a given situation.

3. *Context is independent of the sensing mechanisms.* Even though context information is usually gathered automatically, the representation of this information should be independent of the sensing mechanism. As we will see in the following sections, if our context model is tightly coupled to the sensing hardware, the system evolution will be heavily compromised.

In order to fulfill these requirements, we decided to split context in a set of *context aspects*, each one responsible for modeling the behavior of a specific context feature. As a result, the context is not seen as data provided by external acquisition mechanisms, but as the emergent behavior provided by the interaction of the different context aspects. This behavior, encapsulated in every context aspect, varies as the application runs, allowing to provide different adaptation to the user according to his context. By using this scheme, what we are actually modeling is the behavior that is contextually relevant to the user in a given moment of time.

4   The Object-Oriented Architecture

As previously mentioned, to achieve flexible context-aware applications a set of main concepts must be identified and clearly separated. Other approaches for building context-aware applications have also identified concerns that must be separated to achieve modularity: sensing (implemented for example as Widgets in [4]), interpretation (also mentioned as context management in [9]) and application model. Layered architectural approaches [9], or MVC-based ones like [14] provide the basis for separating those concerns using simple and standard communication rules. However, applications are considered as being monolithic artifacts that deserve little or no attention. It is easy to see in the motivating example that the gap between application objects (in particular their behaviors) and the outer (context-related) components is not trivial.

As a case study, let's analyze the location aspect of the example in greater detail. Context-aware applications are supposed to aid the user during his daily activities, which means that they must be able to cope with location models of different granularity; for example, if we want to offer a set of services in the user's office, small distances are important and a fine-grained location model should be used. On the other hand, if we want to offer services when the user is moving in his car along the country, the granularity of the location model must be larger, so that adaptation can be provided according to the user's activity. Unfortunately, there is no silver bullet for location models and we must use different location representation according to the specific requirements.

Symbolic models [11] that represent inclusion, adjacencies or distances between locations characterized as symbols are generally well suited for indoor location. These models represent in a clear way those relationships between the locations, can represent very fine-grained structural arrangements and are easy to understand by humans. On the other hand, Geometric models [11] are well suited for representing large areas where accuracy does matter or when it is necessary to calculate distances between objects with an important level of correctness. As a drawback, creating geometrical models for large maps (for example, a city) is a hard task (when not impossible) without the aid of a specialized organization. Also, geometrical models don't add semantics to the regions they represent, they just provide the boundaries for performing calculations; so, if we want to tag a specific polygon as being the *Plaza Hotel*, we must do it manually.

In this area it's worthwhile mentioning Google Earth and it's Community. This application uses different levels of detail of geometric locations, allowing to easily compute distances between two places, get 3D views of the cities and print maps with country borders. When routing information is available, we can also ask for the shortest route between two places. Although Google Earth doesn't handle symbolic locations, the Community users can tag latitude/longitude points with descriptions in order to give semantic to geometric points. Descriptions can vary from simple strings explaining what the place is, to a complete description with photos and links. Even though tags give semantic to geometric places, they cannot be consider symbolic locations since they don't offer any location information; symbolic locations (and locations in general) must provide meaningful information in order to compute at least one operation by themselves, which is not the case (a tag without the geometric point where it's attached to can't perform any operation).

As can be seen from the example above, a single context aspect (such as the user's location), can turn out to be a whole world in itself. On top of this, the forces that may impose changes in a context aspect have nothing (or very little) to do with the application model or with the services that are provided. For example, when adapting the user services to his location, the services subsystem should only care about knowing *where* the user is (for example, in the library) and not about the details of *how* the location model determines the user's location. Also, we should remember that context is essentially dynamic and that context aspects can't be fixed at design time. For this reasons, in the same way that MVC [10] architectures argue for a clear separation between the model and the view, we argue that a similar separation must hold between the application model, the context model, how the context is sensed and the way services are offered to the user.

4.1   Main Components

In order to tackle the issues previously mentioned, we decided to decompose a context-aware application in two orthogonal views: the application-centered view and the sensing view. The application-centered view is concerned with context and service management and is in turn separated in three layers. The sensing view (which will be described in Section 5) is concerned with the mechanisms used to get external data and how to feed this data, as transparent as possible, into the context aspects. In Fig. 1 we show the layers that comprise the application centered view.

In the **Application Model** layer we specify the application classes with their "standard" behavior (i.e. those application classes and methods are not aware of the user's context, neither they exhibit context-related information). In our example this layer would have classes like `Room`, `Schedule`, `Teacher`, and so on. The **Context** layer is in turn composed of a set of context aspects, each one creating a high-level representation of a specific part of the user's context. As can be seen in Fig. 1, we take a different approach when it comes to establishing the relationship between the application and the context model: in most approaches, context is presented as data that is somehow processed by the application, thus creating a knowledge relationship from the core application to the context representation. As explained in the previous section, we consider that this approach is rather limited and that a behavioral point of view should be taken to handle context. In our architecture the application does not fetch data from the context, but it is the context itself who extends the application functionality. By separating context in independent aspects we are able to add the behavior that is contextually relevant in a given moment, so that it is the aspect itself the one who decides how the adaptation is made.

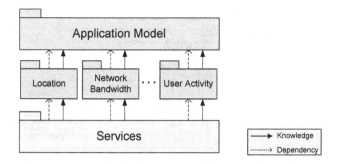

Fig. 1. A layered approach for the Application-Centered view

The **Services** layer models the concepts related to a context-aware application from a services point of view. This layer has the responsibility of deciding what services are available to the user in a given situation. For that purpose, four main abstractions are modeled: the user, the services, the services environment and the service providers. As expected, the user object represents the physical user who is carrying a mobile device and which is the focus of the system's attention. The user in this layer has attached a set of context aspects that can vary dynamically, according to what is considered contextually relevant in a given time. When there is a change in the user's context (either because a context aspect changed or because a context aspect is added or removed) the user's available services are updated according to the system configuration. This configuration basically establishes a relationship between the services and the different contexts in which the user may be, generally represented as a constraint (i.e. a certain service is provided if a constraint is satisfied). As an example, when working with location-dependent services, each service will be associated with a set of geographic areas represented in the location aspect; when the user changes his location, new services may become active or former ones removed.

Each service is associated with a service provider, which is in charge of creating the service when required, acting as a Builder [7]. Besides, every service provider defines a set of constraints to determine when it is allowed to give its services to the user. Upon a change in the user's context, each provider is asked to reevaluate his constraint in order to determine if a new set of services should be added to the user or existing ones removed. Finally, services, providers and users are immersed in a service environment, which reifies the real-world environment from a services view. The service environment acts a Mediator [7] between service providers, services and users.

4.2   Communication Mechanisms

As shown in Fig. 1, we use a layered approach to separate the application-centered view concerns. In this view, context aspects are the basis on which the services layer is mounted. In the services layer, the user object holds the set of currently active context aspects, which are used to determine what services

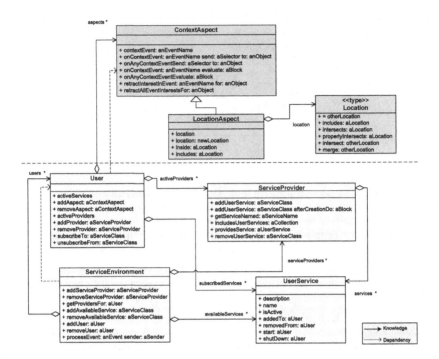

Fig. 2. Relationships between services and context aspects

are available at a given time. As we mentioned earlier, in order to improve evolution, context aspects should be decoupled from the services layer, which is accomplished by making an extensive use of the dependency mechanism. Fig. 1 shows how the Service layer is dependent of every context aspect, so that it can get a notification when there is a context change. If we dig a little inside the services layer we will see that the relationship is established between the user and the services: every user has a collection of context aspects, which he is in turn dependent of. When there is a change in a context aspect the user gets the corresponding notification. This notification is in turn propagated to the environment (again, using the dependency mechanism) which is in charge of triggering the service providers re-evaluation. In order to establish dependencies we originally used the standard notification mechanism, but as the system grew in complexity we decided to implement our own event subsystem. To do so, we modeled a set of events, handlers and adaptors to easily trigger context changes and configure the system response to those changes. In Fig. 2 we show a class diagram depicting these relationships, using Location as a concrete example of a context aspect.

4.3   Creating, Deploying and Activating Context-Aware Services

Creating New Services. New services are defined as subclasses of the abstract class UserService and thus a specific instantiation of a service is an object that plays the role of a Command [7]. The specific service's behavior is defined by overriding appropriate methods of UserService such as *#addedTo: aUser* (triggered when the service is made available to the user), *#start* (triggered when the users selects the service form the available services list), and so on. For example, a service that presents the course's material in the room where a lecture is taking place would be defined as a subclass of Service, and the message *#setUp: aUser* would search in the schedule for the appropriate objects to display.

Subscribing to Services. In order to access the services supplied by a service provider, the user must subscribe to those services he is interested in. Once he is subscribed, when the constraints imposed by the provider are met (e.g. being in a particular location at a certain time), the services are made available to the user. In our model, the service environment knows which services are registered, and therefore the users can query the environment for existing services to subscribe. Besides, when new services are added to the environment, a change notification is broadcasted to the users so that they can take the proper action according to the configuration they state. The default action is to show a visual notification (a small icon) indicating that new services are available, but the user may decide to configure the system to ignore notifications or to automatically get subscribed to any new service that appears. It's interesting to notice that this functionality is provided by a standard service which has the environment as its model.

Registering Services in Specific Providers. To provide context-awareness and to avoid the use of large rule sets, services are associated with (registered to) specific providers. When the user's context satisfies the provider's constraints, all services registered to that provider (to which the user has subscribed) are made available. By using the concept of service providers, the architecture also achieves the desired independence from the sensing mechanism, i.e. the circumstances under which the services are made available to the user don't belong to the scope of a sensing device (e.g. receiving a beacon signal) but to logical constraints. These logical constraints can be specified programmatically or interactively: they can be obtained by applying a set of operators to specific context concepts (for example, in the case of working with the location aspect, the operation may involve rooms, corridors, etc) or defined arbitrarily in terms of the user preferences (which can involve any context aspect).

As an example, suppose that we want to offer a location service in which a map appears showing where the user is standing. Clearly, we would expect this service to be available in the university building or even in the entire campus. If we are working with symbolic location we would probably have a "Building" location as the parent of the location tree that encompasses the rooms inside the building. So, in order to provide the location service for the building, we would create a new service area that is associated with the "Building" location; with this configuration, when the user enters the building (and as long as he is inside of it) he will have that service available. Now suppose that we would like to extend this service to the entire campus; using our approach we would just need to change the area covered by the service area (i.e., changing the restriction

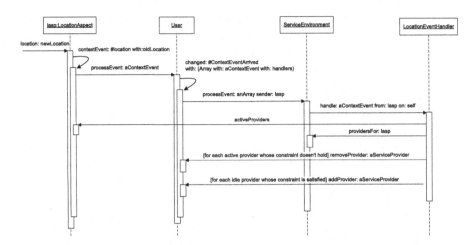

Fig. 3. Updating services as a response to a change in the location aspect

of the service provider), which in case of symbolic location means changing the location "Building" to "University Campus". It is important to notice here that the location constraint is not expressed in terms of sensing information, but in terms of the location model.

Service Activation. When the user's context changes (for example, as he moves in a location-aware environment), it triggers a notification event that reaches a User instance in the Service layer. Then, this object interacts with its environment to determine if a previously inactive service provider should be active, or if a currently active provider should be removed. In case a new provider is added to the user's active ones, the corresponding services are made available to him according to his subscriptions. As mentioned before, a service is presented to a user if it is available in an active provider and if the user is subscribed to it. A subset of these interactions is shown in Fig. 3 by means of a UML sequence diagram, where the location aspect is used as an example.

4.4 Context as Behavior Added to the User

In Section 3 we presented a context model in which context was represented in terms of behavior and not data. From the application point of view, context aspects were seen as software modules that added new behavior to the core application, using this core functionality when needed. From the services point of view, context aspects are responsible for deciding when a given service can be provided to the user. Since the service model is user-centered, the context aspects are applied to the user itself, which is modeled in the service layer by the User class.

As we stated earlier, each context aspect represents a unit of behavior that is contextually relevant to the user in a given moment. From that point of view, when a new context aspect is added to the user, the user's behavior is extended with the behavior provided by the context aspect. So, apart from the behavior defined in the User class, each particular instance of User will behave according to his currently available context aspects. Achieving this kind of functionality is easy in Smalltalk, since we can rely on the *#doesNotUnderstand:* message to forward the message send to the available context aspects. Of course, as with multiple inheritance, there is a problem if more than one context aspect implements the same message. This conflict can be tested when a new context aspect is added to the user and raise a notification in case of conflict. Although this solution is not optimal it turned out to be quite handy in practice. As a second choice, the sender of the message can ask for a given aspect and specify explicitly who should receive the message, very much like the Role Object [3] pattern.

5   Handling Different Sensing Mechanisms

As explained in Section 4.1, our architecture is decomposed in two views: the application-centered view, which has already been explained, and the sensing view, which is in charge of feeding sensor data to the context aspects. Since the idea of a context-aware application is to give functionality to the user in a transparent way, context information must be gathered automatically (i.e. sensed). To make matters worse, hardware devices used for this purpose are usually non-standard, and the data these devices deliver is often far from what an applications needs: while sensed data is represented as strings, numbers or pairs, our applications are built in terms of objects. For these reasons, we consider context sensing as an important architectural problem. In order to tackle it, we have developed a modular design so that changes in the sensing features don't impact in the application. We based our design on the fact that the context model and the way it is sensed are of different nature. In a context-aware application several sensors may be used for determining information about a single context aspect, and, at the same time, a single sensor's data may be used in many ways for inferring information on different context aspects.

As an example consider a user moving with his PDA inside a building. To detect where the user is standing, we can take advantage of the Bluetooth receiver in his PDA and place a Bluetooth beacon in every room. Each beacon can send different room IDs, which will be interpreted to know what the user's location is. Now suppose there are billboards hanging on the walls inside the building, which we would like to enhance with digital services (for example, showing the web-version of the billboard, or having the chance to leave digital graffiti). In order to do this we can use an infrared beacon to capture the user's location, this time with a finer granularity than the one provided by the Bluetooth beacon and with the added value that we know the user is effectively pointing at the billboard, since infrared signals are directional. In this example, the location of the user is being sensed by two different devices at the same time, one giving more detailed information than the other. As a second example consider the case when the user is not carrying the receiving sensor; for instance, suppose that the user is wearing a Bat unit [8] that constantly sends a unique identifier. This identifier is captured by the receiver units placed on the ceiling of the rooms to calculate the user's location. In order to use this system we need a mechanism that allows us to monitor the user's location, even though the value is being sensed by an external receiver. This means that the context model should be independent of the physical location of the sensors; it shouldn't matter whether the sensors are attached to the PDA or placed on the room's ceiling.

The examples presented above shows that the way context is represented and the way it is sensed belong to different concerns. This is why, as shown in Fig. 4, we consider sensing as a concern that cross-cuts the context aspects layer.

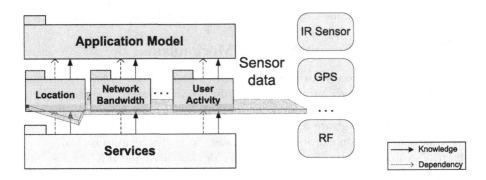

Fig. 4. Sensing as a cross-cutting concern

In order to decouple context modeling from acquisition, our architecture adds a layer between the hardware devices and the context model (see Fig. 5). The basic abstraction in this layer is the sensing aspect (modeled in the `SensingAspect` class), which is basically an object that watches over a hardware sensor and reacts to every new data arrival. To implement this, it has a policy that determines whether the values should be pulled or pushed from the sensor. When creating a new sensing aspect, programmers must provide the message to be sent to the context model when sensed data changes. To improve this task, we have created pluggable sensing aspects that can be configured with a block, and adaptable sensing aspects that take a message to be performed, pretty much like the standard `AspectAdaptor` and `PluggableAdaptor` from the Wrapper GUI framework. In case a more sophisticated behavior is needed, the programmer can create his own `SensingAspect` subclass.

Another important issue when using sensors is to decide whether every signal must be sent to the application or not. In some cases we won't need to forward all the information that sensors deliver, avoiding cluttering the application with

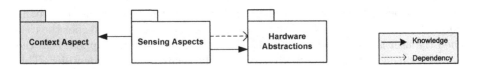

Fig. 5. Layered approach for the Sensing view

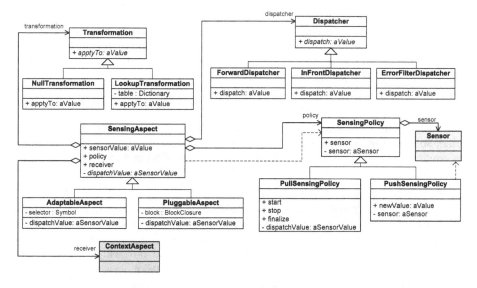

Fig. 6. Class diagram of the sensing aspects package

constant notifications. As an attempt to solve this problem we have introduced the notion of dispatchers (represented in the abstract class `Dispatcher`) that has the responsibility of deciding which signals are let into the system. For example, an `ErrorFilterDispatcher` would be in charge of filtering those signals whose noise level is beyond a given threshold. To complete the process of gathering information from sensors and feeding it to the context model we need to solve the mismatch between sensors' data and applications' needs. To address this problem, we have created the `Transformation` abstract class. Transformations are intended to convert atomic values delivered by sensors to full fledged objects which will feed the context aspect. This transformation can range from simple table lookups to complex machine reasoning processes. Fig. 6 shows the complete class diagram of the Sensing Aspects package.

6   A Pure Object-Based Distribution Scheme

Context-aware applications generally need to share information between a set of devices. This not only encompasses sensing devices (e.g. a server that publishes information gathered by a weather station located in the building) but different kind of services (e.g. location-aware messengers and reminders, shared virtual folders, friend finders, etc.). For this reason we need a mechanism to distribute the proposed architecture between a set of devices and let them share the information they need. Since we can't expect to know the characteristics of every device beforehand or the connection speed between any two devices, the distribution mechanism shouldn't impose a fixed communication schema between the devices; as a matter of fact it should allow objects to *live* in different machines as needed. As an example let's consider again the user and his location aspect and let's analyze how these objects can be distributed considering that the user emits his unique *id* using the Bluetooth port of his PDA. If we decide to move the whole computation to the client device, we would model the external Bluetooth receiver as a Proxy [7] linked to the machine that is physically connected to the Bluetooth receiver. Each time the desktop machine receives a new signal it will forward the received value to the client, which will then process it as explained in the previous sections. On the other hand, if the client device can't handle this kind of computation, we should move as much as we can to the desktop machine, so that the information arrives as processed as possible. In this example we could move the whole dispatching process to the desktop machine, so that the client only receives an update when his location has changed (notice that this also means saving network bandwidth). Following this idea we could take this a step further and move the whole location aspect to the desktop machine, which would be represented in the client machine as a proxy to the real object residing in a remote machine. This means that each time the user changes his location there would be a remote computation to find out which services are added or removed, and as a result the instance of the User class residing in the client device would receive the *#addService:* or *#removeService:* message. Of course this last strategy implies a big risk: if the user gets out of the wi-fi range or the network goes down he loses all location information.

In order to cope with the distribution concern we decided to use the Opentalk [17] framework and extend it to cover our needs. In the next section we will give a brief review of the framework and then explain the extensions we've made so far.

6.1 Opentalk Basics

Opentalk [17] is a distribution framework for VisualWorks that gives flexible support for the development of distributed applications. To achieve this, Opentalk is organized in a series of layers, which includes communication protocols, object services, brokers and remote objects. The Opentalk Communication Layer provides the basic abstractions for developing the connection protocols. These protocols can operate on top of TCP/IP or UDP transport layers. In particular, our work is based on TCP/IP, using the built-in support for Smalltalk-to-Smalltalk interoperability.

In our framework we have exploited the cross-platform nature of the Visual-Works implementation to manage the issue of heterogeneous networks imposed by mobile systems. Thanks to the different VMs available we are able to support several operating systems running over separate hardware platforms (we are currently working on Linux, Windows 2000 and XP on desktops and Windows CE and Mobile on Pocket PC). A VisualWorks image can run almost identically on any supported platform[1], thus allowing the arrangement of a heterogeneous network.

---

[1] In the case of Win CE or Windows Mobile deployment, we have to take into account also those issues concerning the graphical user interface and display screen size (such as a proper Look-&-Feel and a minimal and convenient layout of visual components). In addition, the processor speed of the target machine and the memory footprint of the deployed image must be taken into an account if we want the final application to run decently.

Request Broker and Remote Messaging. Opentalk provides a complete request broker implementation, which is combined with the Smalltalk reflective capabilities to provide transparent remote communication between Smalltalk images. The communication between objects residing in different environments (images) depends on the functionality provided by those brokers. In order to be remotely accessible, an object must be exported through a local broker, which in turn assigns an object identifier (oid) and registers the recent exported object on an internal table. Once the object has been exported, any remote object containing a proper reference to this object, can collaborate with him by directly sending normal messages. This transparency is achieved thanks to the use of generic proxies (discussed in the following section). However, before any two objects can remotely communicate, it is necessary to resolve the initial reference between the two hosting images (i.e. between both request brokers), which can be easily achieved by exporting a root object with a predefined name. Once this is solved, subsequent communication is done transparently due to the inherent characteristic of navigation by reachability and the use of proxies in conjunction with the underlying machinery provided by the brokers.

The internal structure of the brokers is a bit complex, since it collaborates with many different kind of objects to effectively allow for remote message interchange. Among the main collaborators we can mention the `ObjectAdaptor`, `Listener`, `Transport` and `Marshaller`. The object adaptor is in charge of registering those objects that have been exported through the broker and to coordinate listeners and transports. The listener is constantly waiting for new connection requirements incoming from other hosts. When one of this requirements arrives, the listener accepts it and creates a new transport (i.e., a new transport is created for every connection between brokers). Every transport is in turn bound to a specific socket and works as the entry point for receiving and delivering remote messages. In order to accomplish this task an encoding procedure must be done, so that remote message sends can be converted to a binary representation (i.e. a byte array). This procedure (known as marshalling) is performed by the marshaller, who is in charge of transforming remote messages into transport packets. Each transport will collaborate with his own marshaller and will use his services to encode and send messages and to receive and decode them.

To mimic the message sends in the local images, brokers use a synchronic communication policy. The broker that is in charge of dispatching outgoing messages (an instance of `STSTRequest`) will send the remote message and wait for the response (an instance of `STSTReply`). This message send will cause that in the image where the actual object is residing a local message will be send, faking the remote invocation as a local one. Once the message has been dispatched, the sending image will be waiting until a response arrives or a time period expires. If the response arrives, the returning object is decoded and control is passed back to the object that originally sent the message.

Remote Objects and Proxies. A remote proxy [7] is a local representative for an object (its *subject*) that resides in a different address space. When a message is sent to the proxy, it automatically forwards it to its subject and waits for its response. Thus, from the sender point of view, there is no difference between working with local or remote objects[2].

In Opentalk, the `RemoteObject` class performs the role of remote proxy and maintains an indirect reference to its subject by using an instance of `ObjRef`, which is basically composed of a socket address (i.e. an IP address + a port number) and an object identifier (also known as *oid*). When an instance of `RemoteObject` receives a message, it forwards the request to its subject by means of the `#doesNotUnderstand:` mechanism; for this purpose the proxy leans on the broker's services, which is responsible for deliver the message through the network. Also, whenever an object is exported (i.e. passed by reference[3]) from one image to another, a new proxy is created to represent the remote object. This instantiation task is responsibility of the local broker.

In Opentalk the concrete `RemoteObject` class is a subclass of `Proxy`, which is a special abstract class that does not understand any messages. The `RemoteObject` class automatically forwards those messages that does not understand, leading to a generic implementation of a remote proxy. This basic implementation allows us to apply seamless distribution to any existing application with relative little effort. Therefore, we can postpone this decision until last moment (or when considered necessary) without worring about distribution issues on early stages of system development. However there are some trade-offs that we must be taken into consideration when working with this kind of distribution technique, in particular when dealing with mobile systems. In the first place, the proxy generally implies an important network traffic, since messages are constantly flowing through the network. Also, this approach needs a constant connection between the images where the proxy and the subject are, not being well suited to distribute objects in networks with intermittent connections. Also, even though we can assume having a continuous connection, in mobile applications we expect the user to be moving around large spaces. As a consequence, accessing the host where the subject resides can be fast in a given time, but extremely slow if the user has moved to a place where the connection to access that host is slow. In these cases, we would like to be able to move the subject to a host that can be accessed with less network delay. Hence, we are motivated to figure out how to take the maximum advantage of this approach and combine it with new alternatives in order to cope with these issues.

Pass Modes and Distribution Strategies. Opentalk provides a fixed set of general purpose object pass modes which indicates how an object will be distributed across images: by reference, by value, by name and by oid. A pass mode can be seen as a strategy for object distribution, because it decides the way in which an object should be distributed when exported to another host; therefore, we will use interchangeably the terms pass mode and distribution strategy. For the sake of conciseness (and because pass by name and pass by oid

---

[2] There is a subtle issue regarding object identity and pass modes that we will not address due to space reasons.

[3] As we will see in the next section, there are many ways of distributing objects.

modes are not frequently used) we are going to describe the two most relevant pass modes: by reference and by value. The first one is the basic proxy approach: the subject resides in a single image and the other images have proxies that refer to the subject. On the other hand, passing an object by value means that a copy is sent to the requesting image. It is important to notice that this distribution policy does not guarantee that both objects will be consistent; as a matter of fact, passing an object by value is like creating a local copy, and then moving it to another image, so future messages sends may alter their structures without any restrictions or implicit synchronization.

The way an object will be passed can be decided at the class or instance level. In order to indicate the pass mode of all the instances of a given class, the *#passMode* message must be redefined in the desired class (by default all objects are passed by reference). If we want to specify how a specific instance should be passed across the net, the *#asPassedByReference* or *#asPassedByValue* messages can be sent to the specific instance. Sending any of these messages will end up creating an instance of `PassModeWrapper` on the receiver, which will mask the original pass mode defined in the object's class.

As we stated before, we found Opentalk proxy distribution mechanism to be very well suited, especially because of the transparency it provides. On the other hand, in order to accommodate to mobile environments, we found it necessary to enhance the framework to provide new distribution policies, which are explained in the next section.

6.2   Opentalk Extensions

In order to accommodate our needs we devised a series of extensions to the Opentalk framework. These extensions include traceability, migration and object mirroring. In order to clarify the ideas that will be covered in this section we briefly explain the main concepts:

- Traceability is the capability that an object has of knowing all the remote references that have him as a subject. This can be seen as asking an object for all his remote owners.
- We refer to replicas when we talk about a copy of some object that resides in a different Smalltalk image. This doesn't mean that there is any kind of connection between the original object and the replica; a replica is just a copy of the object with no synchronization mechanisms.
- Migration means moving an object from one image to another. This movement must be consistent and rearrange any remote reference to update its address to the new host (note that local references can be easily converted by using the *#become:* message, while remote ones will require a more sophisticated mechanism).
- Mirroring refers to having an object replicated in a way that the replicas are consistent. So, if an object is modified in an image, all the distributed mirrors are modified to maintain the consistency.

As we will see, by adding these features, we can distribute objects in new ways and have a flexible base to dynamically change distribution policies to adapt to context changes.

Extensible Pass Mode Hierarchy. The first task we had to accomplish was a redesign of the way pass modes where modeled. In the original framework, pass modes where represented by a symbol (i.e. #reference, #value, #name, #oid), making it impossible to delegate behavior to the pass modes themselves. To solve this issue, pass modes are now represented as first-class objects and modeled by a class hierarchy rooted at the `PassMode` class. Thanks to this first modification we obtained a flexible way to add new pass modes. The basic pass modes are represented by the classes `PassByReferenceMode`, `PassByValueMode`, `PassByNameMode` and `PassByOIDMode`. Each of these classes redefines the abstract method *#marshal:on:* which uses double dispatch to delegate the specific encoding of the object to a marshaller.

In order to facilitate the creation of new pass modes, the `CustomPassMode` class is defined to act as an abstract class. This class redefines the *#marshal:on:* message to provide a Template Method [7], so that new pass modes only need to redefine their specific features. This class is the root that we used to define the new pass modes.

Traceability. Traceability is defined as the capability that an object has of knowing all the remote references that have him as a subject. This is achieved by knowing those places to which it was exported and then tracking those remote proxies that are referencing it. Traceability is implemented as a special type of passing an object by reference and is modeled by the `TraceablePassMode` class.

When a *traceable* object is exported, a local wrapper (`TraceableObjectWrapper`) is created to hold a collection of the remote proxies that are referencing the target object in other hosts; we will refer to this original object as a *primary copy*. When a host requests for a proxy to the primary copy, instead of creating a remote object, an instance of `TraceableRemoteObject` is instantiated in the remote host. This object acts basically like a standard remote object, but adds the necessary behavior to notify the primary copy that a new reference to it has been created and to notify it when the proxy has been garbage collected in order to remove the reference. These notifications are really captured by the wrapper created on the primary copy, which is responsible for keeping the remote references collection.

As we will see in the next sections, by adding traceability we can choose between the interested hosts (i.e., hosts that have a remote reference to the primary copy) to mirror or migrate the primary copy. Also, things like distributed garbage collection by reference counting can be easily implemented by adding the required logic on top of the traceability mechanism.

Migration. As was introduced earlier, an object can be replicated in many other images. Once these replicas are created there is no synchronization between the original object and the remote replicas. To perform this remote copy, a

`Replicator` object is introduced. This object is in charge of coordinating the hosts involved in the copy process, which can be triggered explicitly or by defining a set of events related to the environment. In order to fulfill his task, a replicator uses a Strategy [7] that allows to configure how a replica will be made. The most basic one is the `PlainReplication` strategy, which just makes a copy of the object in another image. A more interesting one is the `MigrateAndRedirect` strategy, which migrates the primary copy to another image and rearranges all the remote references to update their information about the host that now holds the object. Also, during this process, all message sends to the primary copy are temporarily frozen so that no inconsistencies can arise.

The migration mechanism was originally needed in order to give the user flexibility when working with portable devices (such as PDAs or smartphones) and desktop computers. Imagine that the user is working in his desktop using his favorite context aware application. Suddenly, a reminder appears notifying that he must go to the airport to catch his flight. Now the user asks his application to shut down, but before doing so, the application tries to find the user's PDA in the network. In case it does, it launches the application by executing a shell command and migrates all his primary copies. As a result, the user automatically has the same up-to-date information in his PDA, with the additional benefit that any remote reference will be properly updated to reflect the host migration of the primary copy (of course, assuming that the PDA has a global connection to the net).

Mirroring (Synchronized Replicas). In contrast with the plain replication, the mirroring mechanism allows to keep a set of replicated objects in a consistent state (i.e. if an instance variable of one of the objects is updated, the remote replicas are updated to be consistent with the object). Associated to this mechanism, three new distribution policies are implemented[4]: `ForwarderPassMode`, `MirrorPassMode` and `StubPassMode`. An object that is exported under any of these three new pass modes can be dynamically changed to any of the other (e.g. an object passed in *forwarder* mode can be changed dynamically to be exported in *mirror* mode). Next we present a brief description of each strategy:

Forwarder. An object exported under this pass mode will forward every message to the primary copy, behaving like an object passed by reference. The added value of this class is the ability of dynamically changing the distribution policy to mirror or stub my receiving the messages *#becomeMirror* or *#becomeStub*.

Mirror. An object exported as a mirror will create copies of himself in the other images, making sure that all the replicas are consistent with the original object. In order to keep this consistency, a mirror object delegates the synchronization mechanism to a Strategy [7], which can be specified at the class or the instance level. At the moment we have implemented two synchronization mechanisms:

---

[4] These set of passing modes are inspired in the distribution strategies used by Gem-Stone.

- A simple one, that just forwards the change to every replica. This strategy doesn't check if the update has been done in a consistent way, assuming an optimistic update. Note that this can easily end up in desynchronized objects in the case that mirrors of the same object are updated at the same time in different images.
- A two-phase strategy, that ensures the objects consistency. In the first phase, the object whose internal state has been updated triggers a notification that will cause the blocking of every mirror by asking for his lock. If all the locks can be successfully obtained, the change is propagated and the objects are unlocked. In the case that the lock can't be obtained a rollback is performed.

In order to support mirrors in a transparent way the immutability and modification management mechanism present in VisualWorks is used. This mechanism allows tagging an object as immutable so that a change in his state triggers an exception. We use the **ModificationManagement** package to have a simpler way of handling changes, by creating a subclass of `ModificationPolicy` (`MirroringPolicy`) which triggers the mirror updates.

Stub. A stub can be seen as a special kind of proxy, that waits until someone sends a message to it. When this happens, the stub gets replaced by a mirror, creating in this way the notion of a lazy-mirror. In order to perform this, the stub sends to himself the message *#becomeMirror* and then re-evaluates the message that was originally sent to him. As expected, a stub can be sent the messages *#becomeMirror* or *#becomeForwarder*.

Dynamic Change of Distribution Policies. Distribution policies can be changed in two granularity levels: at the class level, by redefining the *#passMode* message and at the instance level by using an instance of `PassModeWrapper`. As an extension to this basic mechanism, a family of distribution policies that can be changed dynamically has been introduced (`Forwarder`, `Mirror` and `Stub`), allowing to change the way that mirrors are synchronized. With these tools at our hand, not only can distribution be made transparent to the programmer, but we can also decide what is the best way to distribute a given object. As an example, consider an object in a context-aware system whose instance variables are constantly being updated. If this object is distributed by mirroring, we should expect to have an important network traffic and system unresponsiveness, since every modification implies a locking and an update. On the other hand, if we distribute this object by using a forwarder, the network traffic will be proportional to the messages sends to the primary copy and not to the instance variable update ratio. Of course, this can in turn become a bottleneck, since many hosts would be sending messages to a single image and asking for those messages to be resolved remotely. In order to overcome this issue, we can even use a mixture of distribution policies to balance the charge in a host: the primary copy can be mirrored in a small number of hosts, and then be distributed to the rest of the hosts by using forwarders. In this way, the load is distributed among the hosts that have the mirrors.

7   Related Work

From the conceptual point of view, we found our model of context to fit quite well the ideas presented by Dourish [5]. While in most approaches context is treated as a collection of data that can be specified at design time and whose structure is supposed to remain unaltered during the lifetime of the application, Dourish proposes a phenomenological view in which context is considered as an emergent of the relationship and interaction of the entities involved in a given situation. Similarly, in our approach, context is not treated as data on which rules or functions act, but it is the result of the interaction between objects, each one modeling a given context concern. This idea is based on the concept of a context aspect, that represents the behavior that is contextually relevant to model in a specific situation.

From an architectural point of view, our work can be rooted to the Context Toolkit [4] which is one of the first approaches in which sensing, interpretation and use of context information is clearly decoupled. We obviously share this philosophy though we expect to take it one step further, attacking also the application concerns. Hydrogen [9] introduces some improvements to the capture, interpretation and delivery of context information with respect to the seminal work of the Context Toolkit. However, both fail to provide cues about how application objects should be structured to seamlessly interact with the sensing layers. Our approach proposes a clear separation of concerns between those object features that are context-free, those that involve context-sensitive information (like location and time) and the context-aware services. By placing these aspects in separated layers, we obtain modular applications in which modifications in one layer barely impact in others. To achieve this modular architecture we based on the work of Beck and Johnson [2] in the sense that the sum of our micro-architectural decisions (such as using dependencies or decorators) also generate a strong, evolvable architecture.

Schmidt and Van Laerhoven [15] proposed a middleware architecture for the acquisition of sensor-based context information, which is separated in four different layers: sensors, cues, context and application. The sensors layer is where both physical (such as cameras or active badges) and logical sensors (like system time) are located. Data obtained from sensors is processed by cues on the next layer, whose main function is to synthesize and abstract sensor data by using different statistical functions. Values generated by cues are buffered in a tuple space, which provides for inter-layer communication between the cues layer and the context layer; then, the context layer can read this values and take the appropriate actions. In this approach, the use of middleware architectures helps decoupling the sensing hardware from context abstractions. Our approach also places sensing mechanisms into a separate module, but it does not depend directly on any other; it is treated as a crosscutting concern of the context model, what makes it less sensitive to system changes.

Other approaches that have been presented pay closer attention to monitoring resources and consider adaptation in terms of network bandwidth, memory or battery power. Among these works we can mention Odyssey [12] which was one of the first systems to address the problem of resource-aware adaptation for mobility. In this approach there is a collaborative partnership between the operating system and individual mobile applications, in which the former monitors resource levels and notifies the applications of relevant changes. Then, each application independently decides how to best adapt when notified. This adaptation occurs when the application adjust the fidelity[5] levels of the fetched data. Following a similar path, CARISMA is a middleware model that enables context-aware interactions between mobile applications. The middleware interacts with the underlying operating system and it is responsible for maintaining a representation of the execution context. Context could be internal resources (e.g. memory and battery power), external resources (e.g. bandwidth, network connection, location, etc.) or application-defined resources (e.g. user activity or mood). CARISMA provides an abstraction of the middleware as a customizable service provider, so that a service can be delivered in different ways (using different policies) when requested in different context. On the other hand, MobiPADS presents an event notification model to allow the middleware and applications to perform adaptation and reconfiguration of services in response to an environment where the context varies. Services (known as mobilets) are able to migrate between client and server hosts. MobiPADS supports dynamic adaptation to provide flexible configuration of resources to optimize the operations of mobile applications.

Regarding distribution policies, even though not in the OO paradigm, an interesting work is presented in GSpace [13], which implements a shared data space. This middleware monitors and dynamically adapts its distribution policies to the actual use of the data in the tuple space. The unit of distribution in a shared data space is called tuple, which is an ordered collection of type fields, each of them containing an actual value. Additionally, in GSpace tuples are typed, allowing the association of separate distribution policies with different tuple types. Making an analogy, we use the object as the basic unit of distribution, whose internal state can be seen as the data represented by a tuple. In Smalltalk, an object belongs to a particular class which can be mapped to the notion of type present in GSpace and assign the distribution policy at the class (type) level and change it at run-time. In addition, we provide the functionality to assign distribution policies in an object basis.

8   Concluding Remarks and Further Work

We have presented an architecture for developing context-aware applications that emphasizes in a clear separation of concerns. Also, by using and extending the dependency mechanism to connect different layers we have been able to avoid cluttering the application with rules or customization code that would result in applications that are difficult to maintain.

---

[5] Fidelity is the degree to which data presented at a client matches the reference copy in the server.

From the context modeling point of view, we have shown a behavior-oriented representation, where context is built from different context aspects. Those aspects provide the behavior that is contextually relevant in a given moment. This model, with the flexibility provided by a fully reflective environment as Smalltalk, provides the kind of dynamic adaptation that we consider context-aware applications need. We have also founded many things in common with the MVC architecture when we look at the way that sensing is separated from the context aspects and context aspects from services. This isn't surprising at all, since the reasons and the aims are basically the same: allow different layers of a system to evolve independently, without propagating changes to other layers. Finally, by extending the Opentalk framework we are able to choose between different strategies to distribute objects, making it possible to accommodate the system to the needs of mobile applications.

We are now working in the following issues:

- As mentioned in the introduction, we consider that next-generation context-aware applications will have such an extent that no single company or development group will be able to handle on its own. To cope with this issue, an integration platform is needed to allow software modules created by independent groups to interact seamlessly.
- Characterize object behavioral patterns, so that we can discover general rules for distributing objects with a given distribution policy.
- Adapt distribution policies to context. For example, a context aspect can be used to represent the network bandwidth, so that when it becomes lower than a certain threshold the distribution policy of predefined objects is changed (e.g. from forwarder to mirror to reduce the network traffic).
- Supporting intermittent network connections.
- We started a research track on Human-Computer Interaction, since we found that designing usable context-aware applications is not an easy task. The inherent limitations of mobile devices, such as small screens, tiny keyboards and lack of resources makes the design of usable GUIs rather difficult, so other non-graphical solutions must be explored, like audio or tactile UIs. Additionally, users of context-aware applications tend to be constantly moving and easily distracted, what makes usability a determining factor.

References

1. Gregory D. Abowd. Software engineering issues for ubiquitous computing. In *ICSE '99: Proceedings of the 21st international conference on Software engineering*, pages 75–84, Los Alamitos, CA, USA, 1999. IEEE Computer Society Press.
2. Kent Beck and Ralph E. Johnson. Patterns Generate Architectures. In *ECOOP*, pages 139–149, 1994.
3. D. Bumer, D. Riehle, W. Siberski, and M. Wulf. Role Object Patterns, 1997.
4. Anind Kumar Dey. *Providing Architectural Support for Building Context-Aware Applications*. PhD thesis, Georgia Institute of Technology, 2000.
5. Paul Dourish. What we talk about when we talk about context. *Personal and Ubiquitous Computing*, 8(1):19–30, 2004.

6. Andrés Fortier, Javier Muñoz, Vicente Pelechano, Gustavo Rossi, and Silvia Gordillo. Towards an Integration Platform for AmI: A Case Study, 2006. To be prsented in the "Workshop on Object Technology for Ambient Intelligence and Pervasive Computing", ECOOP 2006, 4/7/2006.

7. Erich Gamma, Richard Helm, and Ralph Johnson. *Design Patterns. Elements of Reusable Object-Oriented Software*. Addison-Wesley Professional Computing Series. Addison-Wesley, 1995.

8. Andy Harter, Andy Hopper, Pete Steggles, Andy Ward, and Paul Webster. The anatomy of a context-aware application. *Wirel. Netw.*, 8(2/3):187–197, 2002.

9. Thomas Hofer, Wieland Schwinger, Mario Pichler, Gerhard Leonhartsberger, Josef Altmann, and Werner Retschitzegger. Context-Awareness on Mobile Devices - the Hydrogen Approach. In *HICSS*, page 292, 2003.

10. Glenn E. Krasner and Stephen T. Pope. A cookbook for using the model-view controller user interface paradigm in Smalltalk-80. *J. Object Oriented Program.*, 1(3):26–49, 1988.

11. U. Leonhardt. *Supporting Location-Awareness in Open Distributed Systems*. PhD thesis, Dept. of Computing, Imperial College, 1998.

12. Brian D. Noble, M. Satyanarayanan, Dushyanth Narayanan, James Eric Tilton, Jason Flinn, and Kevin R. Walker. Agile application-aware adaptation for mobility. In *SOSP '97: Proceedings of the sixteenth ACM symposium on Operating systems principles*, pages 276–287, New York, USA, 1997. ACM Press.

13. Giovanni Russello, Michel R. V. Chaudron, and Maarten van Steen. Dynamic Adaptation of Data Distribution Policies in a Shared Data Space System. In *CoopIS/DOA/ODBASE (2)*, pages 1225–1242, 2004.

14. Daniel Salber, Anind K. Dey, and Gregory D. Abowd. The Context Toolkit: Aiding the Development of Context-Enabled Applications. In *CHI*, pages 434–441, 1999.

15. Albrecht Schmidt and Kristof Van Laerhoven. How to build smart appliances. *IEEE Personal Communications*, pages 66 – 71, 2001.

16. João Pedro Sousa and David Garlan. Aura: an Architectural Framework for User Mobility in Ubiquitous Computing Environments. In *WICSA*, pages 29–43, 2002.

17. Visualworks Opentalk Developer's Guide - Part Number: P46-0135-05.

Unanticipated Partial Behavioral Reflection

David Röthlisberger[1], Marcus Denker[1], and Éric Tanter[2]

[1] Software Composition Group
University of Bern – Switzerland
[2] Center for Web Research/DCC
University of Chile, Santiago – Chile

Abstract. Dynamic, unanticipated adaptation of running systems is of interest in a variety of situations, ranging from functional upgrades to on-the-fly debugging or monitoring of critical applications. In this paper we study a particular form of computational reflection, called *unanticipated partial behavioral reflection*, which is particularly well-suited for unanticipated adaptation of real-world systems. Our proposal combines the dynamicity of unanticipated reflection, *i.e.,* reflection that does not require preparation of the code of any sort, and the selectivity and efficiency of partial behavioral reflection. First, we propose unanticipated partial behavioral reflection which enables the developer to precisely select the required reifications, to flexibly engineer the metalevel and to introduce the meta behavior dynamically. Second, we present a system supporting unanticipated partial behavioral reflection in Squeak Smalltalk, called GEPPETTO, and illustrate its use with a concrete example of a Seaside web application. Benchmarks validate the applicability of our proposal as an extension to the standard reflective abilities of Smalltalk.

1 Introduction

Dynamic adaptation of a running application makes it possible to apply changes to either the structure or execution of the application, without having to shut it down. This ability is interesting for several kinds of systems, *e.g.,* context-aware applications, long-running systems that cannot afford to be halted, or for monitoring and debugging systems on-the-fly. Adaptation can be considered *a priori* by adopting adequate design patterns such as the strategy pattern [1], but such anticipation is not always possible nor is it desirable: potentially many parts of an application may have to be updated at some point. This is an area in which metaobject protocols, by providing *implicit reification* of some parts of an application [2], are very useful [3, 4, 5].

Reflection in programming languages is a paradigm that supports computations about computations, so-called *metacomputations*. Metacomputations and base computations are arranged in two different levels: the *metalevel* and the *base level* [6, 7]. Because these levels are causally connected any modification to the metalevel representation affects any further computations on the base level [8]. In object-oriented reflective systems, the metalevel is formed in terms of metaobjects: a metaobject acts on *reifications* of program elements (execution

W. De Meuter (Ed.): ISC 2006, LNCS 4406, pp. 47–65, 2007.

or structure). If reifications of the *structure* of the program are accessed, then we talk about *structural reflection*; if reifications deal with the *execution* of the program, then we are referring to *behavioral reflection*.

This paper is concerned with a particular form of behavioral reflection, since Smalltalk already supports powerful structural reflective mechanisms. Following the work of McAffer on metalevel engineering [9], we adopt an *operational* decomposition of the metalevel: reifications represent *occurrences* of *operations* denoting the activity of the base program execution. Examples of operations are message sending, method execution, and variable accesses. An occurrence of an operation is a particular event (*e.g.,* a particular sending of a message).

We focus on two particular enhancements of behavioral reflection that make it more appropriate in real-world systems. First, *unanticipated* behavioral reflection (UBR) enables the deployment of metaobjects affecting the behavior of a program while it is already running. This makes it possible to fully support unanticipated software adaptation [4]. Second, an admitted issue of behavioral reflection is its overhead in terms of efficiency: jumping to the metalevel at runtime — reifying current computation and letting a metaobject perform some metalevel behavior — is powerful but costly. *Partial* behavioral reflection (PBR) has been proposed to overcome this issue, by letting users precisely select what needs to be reified, and when [10]. Furthermore, PBR allows for flexible engineering of the metalevel, making it possible to design a *concern-based* metalevel decomposition (*i.e.,* where one metaobject is in charge of one concern in the base application) rather than the typical *entity-based* metalevel decomposition (*e.g.,* one metaobject per object, or one metaobject per class). Hence it is possible to reuse or compose metaobjects of different concerns which greatly eases the engineering of the metalevel [9,10].

In this paper we propose unanticipated partial behavioral reflection (UPBR) which allows us to insert reflective behavior at runtime into a system (the "unanticipated" in this definition). The reifications are precisely selectable in spatial (which occurrences of which operations) and temporal (when those occurrences are reified) dimensions (the "partial" in UPBR). The metalevel behavior is flexibly engineered by means of fine-grained protocols and selection possibilities that supports gathering of heterogeneous execution points (*i.e.,* occurrences of different operations in different classes and methods).

The contributions of this paper are *(a)* a motivation for the need of unanticipated partial behavioral reflection (UPBR), *(b)* an implementation of UPBR in Squeak Smalltalk, called GEPPETTO, *(c)* an illustration of the use of UPBR in the detection and resolution of a performance bottleneck in an application, without the need to actually stop the application. This is unique because the existing proposals of UBR do not fully support PBR, and reciprocally, the existing systems that truly support PBR are not able to provide full UBR.

The paper is organized as follows: in the next section we describe a running example that serves as the baseline for our motivation and illustration of our proposal. Section 3 then discusses existing reflective support in Smalltalk, as well as the MetaclassTalk extension, followed by an overview of proposals for UBR

(Iguana/J) and PBR (Reflex). In Section 4 we describe how we establish an efficient and expressive approach for UPBR in Smalltalk using runtime bytecode manipulation [11]. Section 4.3 is then dedicated to a description of how to use GEPPETTO, the framework providing UPBR in Smalltalk, by solving our running example. We describe the design of GEPPETTO in more detail in Section 5. Section 6 discusses some implementation issues and in Section 7 we report on some benchmarks validating the applicability of GEPPETTO. Section 8 concludes and highlights directions for future work.

2 Running Example

Let us consider a collaborative website (a Wiki), implemented using the Seaside web framework [12]. When under high load, the system suffers from a performance problem. Suppose users are reporting unacceptable response times. As providers of the system, our goal is to find the source of this performance problem and then fix it. First, we want to get some knowledge about possible bottlenecks by determining which methods consume the most execution time. A simple profiler shall be applied to our Wiki application, but it is not possible to shutdown the server to install this profiler. During the profiling our users should still be able to use the Wiki system as usual. Furthermore, once all the necessary information is gathered, the profiler should be *removed* entirely from the system, again without being forced to halt the Wiki. We have also the *strict* requirement to profile the application in its natural environment and context, because unfortunately the performance bottleneck does not seem to occur in a test installation.

To profile method execution we use simple reflective functionalities. We just need to know the name and arguments of the method being executed, the time when this execution started and the time when it finished to gather statistical data showing which methods consume the most execution time. During the analysis of the execution time of the different methods we see that some very slow methods can be optimized by using a simple caching mechanism. We then decide to dynamically introduce a cache for these expensive calculations in order to solve our performance problem.

As we see in this simple but realistic example, the ability to use reflection is of wide interest for systems that cannot be halted but nonetheless require reflective behavior temporarily or permanently. Furthermore, this example proves that an approach to reflection has to fulfill two important requirements to be applicable in such a situation: first, the reflective architecture has to allow *unanticipated installation and removal* of reflective behavior into an application at runtime. A web application or any other server-based application can often not be stopped and restarted to install new functionality. Moreover, the use of reflection cannot be anticipated before the application is started, hence a preparation of the application to support the reflective behavior that we may want to use later is not a valid alternative here. So the reflective mechanisms have to be inserted in an unanticipated manner. Second, in order to be able to use reflection in a durable manner (*e.g.,* for caching) in a real-world situation, the reflective architecture has to be efficient. This motivates the need for *partial* reflection allowing the programmer to precisely choose the places where reflection is really required and hence minimizing the costs for reflection by reducing the amount of costly reifications occurring at runtime. So to sum up, this example requires *unanticipated partial behavioral reflection* to be solved.

3   Related Work and Motivation

As discussed earlier, changing behavior reflectively at runtime is of great interest for all applications and systems that need to run continuously without interruption, such as servers which provide mission-critical applications. It should be possible to analyze and change the behavior of such a system without the need of stopping and restarting it.

We choose the Smalltalk [13] dialect Squeak [14] to implement a dynamic approach to reflection which supports *unanticipated partial behavioral reflection* (UPBR), because Squeak represents a powerful and extensible environment, well-suited to implement and explore the possibilities of UPBR. Before presenting our proposal, we discuss the current situation of reflective support in standard Smalltalk-80 as well as in the MetaclassTalk extension. We also discuss very related proposals formulated in the Java context, both for unanticipated behavioral reflection and for partial behavioral reflection.

3.1   Reflection in Smalltalk-80

Smalltalk is one of the first object-oriented programming languages providing advanced reflective support [15]. The Smalltalk approach to reflection is based on the metaclass model and is thus inherently structural [7]. A metaclass is a class whose instances are classes, hence a metaclass is the metaobject of a class and describes its structure and behavior. In Smalltalk, message lookup and execution are not defined as part of the metaclass however. Instead they are hard-coded in the virtual machine. It is thus not possible to override in a sub-metaclass the method which defines message execution semantics. While not providing a direct model for behavioral reflection, we can nevertheless change the behavior using the message-passing control techniques presented in [16], or method wrappers [17]. Also, the Smalltalk metamodel does not support the reification of variable accesses, so the expressiveness of behavioral reflection in current Smalltalk is limited.

Although reflection in Smalltalk can inherently be used in an unanticipated manner, the existing *ad hoc* support for behavioral reflection in Smalltalk is not efficient and does not support fine-grained selection of reification as advocated by *partial* behavioral reflection (PBR) [10]. For both reasons (limited expressiveness and lack of partiality), we have to extend the current reflective facilities of Smalltalk: this is precisely the aim of this paper.

3.2   Extended Behavioral Reflection in Smalltalk: MetaclassTalk

MetaclassTalk [18, 19, 20] extends the Smalltalk model of metaclasses by actually having metaclasses effectively define the semantics of message lookup and instance variable access. Instead of being hard-coded in the virtual machine, occurrences of these operations are interpreted by the metaclass of the class of the currently-executing instance. A major drawback of this model is that reflection is only controlled at class boundaries, not at the level of methods or operation occurrences. This way MetaclassTalk confines the granularity of selection of behavioral elements towards purely structural elements. As Ferber says in [7]: "metaclasses are not meta in the computational sense, although they are meta in the structural sense".

Besides the lack of fine-grained selection, MetaclassTalk does not allow for any control of the protocol between the base and the metalevel: it is fixed and standardized. It is not possible to control precisely which pieces of information are reified: MetaclassTalk always reifies everything (*e.g.*, sender, receiver and arguments in case of a message send). Recent implementations of the MetaclassTalk model limit the number of effective reifications by only calling the metaclass methods if the metaclass indeed provides changed behavior. But even then, once a metaclass defines a custom semantics for an operation, all occurrences of that operation in all instances of the the class are reified. Hence MetaclassTalk provides a less ad-hoc means of doing behavioral reflection than in standard Smalltalk-80, but with a very limited support for partial behavioral reflection.

3.3   Unanticipated Behavioral Reflection: Iguana/J

Iguana/J is a reflective architecture for Java [4] that supports unanticipated behavioral reflection, and a limited form of partial behavioral reflection.

With respect to unanticipated adaptation, with Iguana/J it is possible to adapt Java applications at runtime without being forced to shut them down and without having to prepare them before their startup for the use of reflection. However to bring unanticipated adaptation to Java, Iguana/J is implemented via a native dynamic library integrated very closely with the Java virtual machine via the Just-In-Time (JIT) compiler interface [4]. This means that the Iguana architecture is not portable between different virtual machine implementations: *e.g.*, the JIT interface is not supported anymore on the modern HotSpot Java virtual machine. Conversely, we aim at providing UPBR for Smalltalk in a portable manner, in order to widen the applicability of our proposal.

With respect to partiality, Iguana/J supports fine-grained metaobject protocols (MOPs), offering the possibility to specify which operations should be reified. However, precise operation *occurrences* of interest cannot be discriminated, nor can the actual communication protocol between the base and metalevels be specified. This can have unfortunate impact on performance, since a completely reified occurrence is typically around 24 times slower than a non-reified one [4].

3.4   Partial Behavioral Reflection: Reflex

A full-fledged model of partial behavioral reflection was presented in [10]. This model is implemented in Reflex, for the Java environment.

Reflex fully supports partial behavioral reflection: it is possible to select exactly which operation *occurrences* are of interest, as well as *when* they are of interest. These spatial and temporal selection possibilities are of great advantage to limit costly reification. Furthermore, the exact communication protocol between the base and metalevel is completely configurable: which method to call on the metaobject, pieces of information to reify, etc. The model of *links* adopted by Reflex, which consists of an explicit binding of a cut (set of operation occurrences) and an action (metaobject), also gives total control over the decomposition of the metalevel: a given metaobject can control a few occurrences of an operation in some objects as well as some occurrences of other operations in possibly different objects. Hence metalevel engineering is highly flexible, which makes it possible to directly support a concern-based metalevel decomposition, and this is precisely what is required to support aspect-oriented programming [10, 21].

The limitation of Reflex however lies in its implementation context: being a portable Java extension, Reflex works by transforming bytecode. Hence, although reflective behavior occurs at runtime, reflective needs have to be anticipated at load time. This means that Reflex does not allow a programmer to insert new reflective behavior affecting already-loaded classes into a running application. Instead, the programmer is forced to stop the application, define the reflective functionality required and to reload the application to insert this metabehavior. Links can be deactivated at runtime, but at a certain residual cost, because the bottom line in Java is that class definitions cannot be changed once loaded.

3.5   Motivation

As we have seen in this section, although unanticipated partial behavioral reflection is highly attractive, no current proposals provide it. Smalltalk-80 is not well-suited for behavioral reflection, MetaclassTalk and provides only a limited possibility of metalevel engineering, Iguana/J has limited partiality and implementation limitations, and Reflex has limited dynamicity. Our proposal, a reflective extension of Squeak supporting UPBR called GEPPETTO, implements the UBR features of Iguana/J and the PBR features of Reflex to form a powerful, open framework for UPBR which extends, enhances and completes the reflective model of Smalltalk in a useful and efficient way.

4   Unanticipated Partial Behavioral Reflection for Smalltalk

We first overview the model of partial behavioral reflection adopted by GEPPETTO, then discuss how we use bytecode manipulation to achieve unanticipation, and then show how partial behavioral reflection can help to solve the problem introduced in Section 2.

4.1   Partial Behavioral Reflection in a Nutshell

GEPPETTO adopts the model of partial behavioral reflection (PBR) presented in [10], which we hereby briefly summarize. This model consists of explicit *links* binding *hooksets* to *metaobjects* (Figure 1).

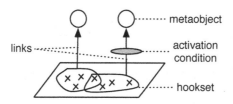

Fig. 1. Links are explicit entities bindings hooksets (at the base level) to metaobjects, possibly subject to activation conditions

A *hookset* identifies a set of related operation occurrences of interest, at the base level. A *metaobject* is a standard object that is delegated control over a partial reification of an operation occurrence at runtime. A *link* specifies the causal connection between a hookset (base level) and a metaobject (metalevel). When occurrences of operations are matched by its hookset, the link invokes a method on the associated metaobject, passing it pieces of reified information. Exactly which method is called, and which pieces of information are passed, is specified in the link itself. So, the link specifies the expected metaobject protocol, and the metaobject can be any object fulfilling this protocol.

Several other attributes further characterize a link, such as the *control* that is given to the metaobject (*i.e.,* that of acting before, after, or around the intercepted operation occurrence). A dynamically-evaluated *activation condition* can also be attached to the link, in order to determine if a link applies or not depending on any dynamically-computable criteria (*e.g.,* the amount of free memory or the precise class of the currently-executing object).

As mentioned earlier, PBR achieves two main goals: *(1)* highly-selective reification, both spatial (which occurrences of which operation) and temporal (thanks to activation conditions), and *(2)* flexible metalevel engineering thanks to fine-grained protocol specification and the fact that a hookset can gather heterogeneous execution points (*i.e.,* occurrences of different operations in different entities).

The following short example illustrates the above definitions. Recall the slow collaborative website mentioned in section 2. To profile this application we introduce dynamically a profiler analyzing the method #toughWork: which we suspect of being responsible for the performance issues. First, we select this method by defining a hookset. This hookset also selects the operation to be reified, in this case the evaluation of the method #toughWork:

```
toughWorks := Hookset inClass: 'WikiCore' inMethod: #toughWork.
toughWorks operation: MethodEval.
```

Second, we specify the link which bridges the gap between the base level (*i.e.,* method #toughWork) and the metalevel (*i.e.,* the metaobject, an instance of class Profiler). The link also describes the call to the metaobject, *i.e.,* which method to invoke on the metaobject, specified by passing a metalevel selector.

```
cache := Link id: #cache hookset: toughWorks metaobject: Profiler new.
cache control: Control around.
cache metalevelSelector: #profile:.
```

After having installed this link by executing cache install the method #profile: of the metaobject will be executed on every call to method #toughWork: of class WikiCore. The developer can provide an arbitrarily complex implementation of the profiler metaobject. See section 4.3 for a more elaborated version of this profiling example.

4.2   Bytecode Manipulation for Unanticipated Behavioral Reflection in Smalltalk

To enable unanticipated partial behavioral reflection in Squeak, the first step is to realize the model for partial reflection as described above. As we have seen in Section 3.1, Smalltalk (and thus Squeak) does not support behavioral reflection properly. To introduce behavioral reflection in a system that does not support it, we can either modify the interpreter (or virtual machine) or transform the code of programs. Modifying the interpreter necessarily sacrifices portability, unless the standard interpreter is actually provided as a sufficiently-*open* implementation.

As Squeak is not implemented using an open interpreter, we use the program transformation approach. We can operate either on source code or on bytecode, but the important thing is, transformation should possibly be done while the program is running. The most appropriate way is arguably to work on bytecode, because it does not require the source code to be present. Squeak by itself does not however support runtime bytecode manipulation appropriately. Fortunately, most of the authors have been involved in BYTESURGEON, a system for runtime bytecode manipulation in Squeak [11].

Following the principles of the implementation of Reflex for Java, we can therefore introduce reflective abilities via insertion of hooks into bytecode. But as opposed to Reflex, in Squeak this can be done at runtime. Since Smalltalk fully supports structural reflection at runtime, and BYTESURGEON extends these structural abilities with method body transformation, we can dynamically introduce selective reflective abilities in running programs.

4.3   Solving the Running Example with Geppetto

To illustrate the use of GEPPETTO, we now explain how to solve the problem introduced in Section 2. In order to find out where the performance issue comes from, we start by elaborating a metaobject protocol to profile the Wiki application. Once we identified the expensive methods that can be cached, we introduce a caching mechanism with GEPPETTO.

Profiling MOP. Defining and introducing dynamically reflective behavior into an application consists of three steps: first, the specification of the places where metabehavior is required (*e.g.,* in which classes and methods, for which objects) by configuring a hookset. Second, the definition of the metaobject protocol (*e.g.,* which data is passed to which metaobject) by setting up one or more links. Third and finally, the installation of the defined reflective functionality.

For profiling method execution times of our Wiki application, we need to define a link, binding the appropriate hookset to a Profiler metaobject. The hookset consists of all method evalution occurrences in all classes of the Wiki application. Hence the hookset is defined as follows:

```
allExecs := Hookset new.
allExecs inPackage: 'Wiki'; operation: MethodEval.
```

All classes of the Wiki package are of interest, and any occurrences of a method evaluation as well.

Now we have to specify which method of the metaobject has to be called, and when. In order to be able to determine the execution time of a method, the profiler acts *around* method evaluations, recording the time at which execution starts and ends, and computing the execution time. The link, called profiler, know the metaobject to invoke, an instance of class Profiler:

```
profile := Link id: #profiler hookset: allExecs metaobject: Profiler new.
profile control: Control around.
```

The profiler therefore needs to receive as parameters the selector being called, the currently-executing instance, and the arguments. Its method to call is thus profileMethod:in:withArguments:. This protocol is described by sending the following message to the profile link:

```
profile metalevelSelector: #profileMethod:in:withArguments:
        parameters: {Parameter selector. Parameter self. Parameter arguments.}
        passingMode: PassingMode plain.
```

The class Parameter is used to describe exactly which information should be reified and how it is passed to the meta level. See Section 5 for more information.

Profiler is a conventional Smalltalk class, whose instances are in charge of handling the task of profiling. For the sake of conciseness, we do not explain the implementation of such a profiler. Finally, to effectively install the link, we just need to execute:

```
profile install.
```

and GEPPETTO inserts all required hooks. From now on, all method executions in the Wiki application get reified and the Profiler metaobject starts gathering data.

Now suppose that based on the gathered data, we determine that a particular method is indeed taking much time: #toughWork: of our Wiki Worker objects. It fortunately happens that this method can seemingly benefit from a simple caching mechanism. We can now completely remove the profiling functionality from the Wiki, going back to normal execution, without reification at all. This is achieve by simply executing:

```
profile uninstall.
```

GEPPETTO then dynamically removes all hooks from the application code, hence further execution is not subject to any extra slowdown at all.

Caching MOP. We now explain how the caching functionality is dynamically added with GEPPETTO. First, we define the hookset, and then the link:

```
toughWorks := Hookset new.
toughWorks inClass: Worker; inMethod: #toughWork:; operation: MethodEval.

cache := Link id: #cache hookset: toughWorks metaobject: Cache new.
cache control: Control around.
cache metalevelSelector: #cacheFor:
        parameters: {Parameter arg1}
        passingMode: PassingMode plain.
```

The sole piece of information that is reified is the first argument passed to the #toughWork: method, denoted with Parameter arg1.

Cache is a Smalltalk class whose instances manage caching (based on single parameter values). In the #cacheFor: method, we first check if the cache contains a value for the passed argument. If so, this value is returned by the metaobject. Else, the metaobject proceeds with the replaced operation of the base level, takes the result answered by this operation via #proceed and returns this value after having stored it into the cache:

```
cacheFor: arg
    | result |
    (self cacheContains: arg) ifTrue: [^self cacheAt: arg].
    result := self proceed.
    self cacheAt: arg put: result.
    ^result
```

In order to be able the to proceed with the original operation the class of the metaobject has to inherit from the generic class ProceedMO. Every instance of subclasses of ProceedMO is allowed to proceed with the replaced operations.

Installing the cache is simply done by executing cache install. GEPPETTO inserts the necessary hooks in the code, and from then on, all evaluations of the #toughWork: method are optimized by caching.

Although this example is pretty straightforward, it illustrates well the point of UPBR: one can easily add reflective features at runtime, with the possibility to completely remove them at any time. This fosters incremental and prototypical resolution of problems such as the one we have illustrated. For instance, if it turns out that the introduced caching is not effective enough, it can be uninstalled, and a more elaborate caching can be devised.

5 Geppetto Design

GEPPETTO instantiates the model of partial behavioral reflection previously presented, as summarized on Figure 2. A link binds a hookset to a metaobject, and is characterized by several attributes. A hookset specifies the operation it matches occurrences of, which can be either MethodEval, MsgSend, InstVarAccess or TempAccess. Hooksets can also be composed as will be explained later.

Spatial selection of operation occurrences in GEPPETTO can be done in a number of ways, as illustrated on Table 1. Eventually, occurrences are selected within method bodies (or boundaries), by applying an *operation selector*, *i.e.*, a predicate that can programmatically determine whether a particular occurrence is of interest or not. Coarser levels of selection are provided to speedup the selection process. First of all, one can eagerly specify the operation of which occurrences may be of interest. Furthermore, one can restrict a hookset to a given package, to a set of classes (using a *class selector*), and/or to a set of methods (using a *method selector*). Convenience methods are provided when an enumerative style of specification is preferred.

Thus far, hooksets are operation-specific. Like in Reflex, GEPPETTO supports hookset composition, so a hookset can match occurrences of different operations. Hooksets can be composed using union, intersection, and difference.

If some hooks of different hooksets conflict with each other, *e.g.*, more than one hookset affects a particular occurrence of a message send in a given method, then these hooks are automatically composed by GEPPETTO. In a composed

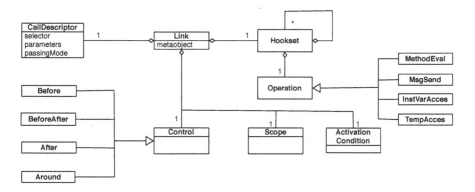

Fig. 2. Class diagram of GEPPETTO design

Table 1. Spatial Selection in GEPPETTO

Selection Level	Example
Package	hookset inPackage: 'Wiki'
Class	hookset classSelector: [:class |class superclass = MyClass]
	hookset inClasses: { MyClass. YourClass. }
Method	hookset methodSelector: [:meth |meth selector = #hello]
	hookset inMethods: { #hello. #bye. }
Operation	hookset operation: MsgSend
Operation Occurrence	hookset operationSelector: [:send | send selector = #size]]

hook every single hook is executed in sequence in the order of their installation time. See Section 6.3 for details about hook composition.

A Link object is created by giving an identifier, the hookset, and by specifying how the metaobject instance(s) are to be obtained.

```
link := Link id: #profiler hookset: hs metaobjectCreator: [ Profiler new ]
```

The block given for the metaobject creator is evaluated to bootstrap metaobject references. As a shortcut, one can directly give a metaobject instance, instead of a block; the given instance will then be shared among entities affected by the link.

A link is further characterized by several attributes:

- Control defines when the metaobject associated to the link is given control over an operation occurrence: it can be either Before, After, BeforeAfter or Around. BeforeAfter means that the metaobject is called *before* and *after* the original operation, whereas Around replaces the operation. The replaced operation then can be executed by calling proceed, if the metaobject is an instance of a subclass of ProceedMO.
- Scope determines the association scheme of a metaobject with respect to base entities. For instance, if the link has object scope, then each instance affected by the link has a dedicated metaobject for the link. The scope can also be *class* (one metaobject per class), or *global* (a unique metaobject for the link).
- an ActivationCondition is a dynamically-evaluated predicate that determines if a link is active (that is, whether reification and delegation to the metaobject effectively occurs). A typical usage of an activation condition is to obtain object-level reifications: the condition can be used as a discriminator of instances that are affected or not by the considered link.
- a CallDescriptor defines the communication protocol with the metaobject. A call descriptor embeds the selector of the message to be sent, the parameters to pass as well as *how* they are passed (*i.e.*, as plain method arguments, packed into an array, or embedded in a wrapper object). Table 2 lists all possible parameters depending on the reified operation.

Finally, for a link to be effective, it has to be dynamically installed by sending the install message to it. At any time, a link can be uninstalled via uninstall. Links

Table 2. Supported reified information

Operation	Reified Data	Description
All Operations	context	execution context
	self	the object
	control	before, after or replace
Message Send/	arguments	arguments as an array
Method Evaluation	argX	X^{th} argument
	sender	sender object
	senderSelector	sender selector
	receiver	receiver object
	selector	selector of method
	result	returned result (after only)
Temp/InstVar Access	name	name of variable
	offset	offset of variable
	value	value of variable
	newvalue	new value (write only)

have identifiers, which can be used to retrieve them from a global repository at any time (Link get: #linkID).

6   Implementation Issues

In this section we explain a crucial part of the implementation of GEPPETTO: the installation of hooks into the bytecode. As explained earlier, we have to dynamically install hooks at runtime to be able to apply reflection in an unanticipated manner into a running system. Therefore, we require a means to manipulate bytecode at runtime. For that purpose we use BYTESURGEON, a framework for runtime manipulation of bytecode in Squeak [11]. Using this tool we do not have to work directly with bytecode. Instead we write our hooks in normal Smalltalk code, which we then pass to BYTESURGEON. Internally, BYTESURGEON will compile our code to bytecode and insert the resulting bytecode into compiled methods.

6.1   Adapting Method Binaries

To adapt the binary code of method, we first select the method in which we want to change the bytecode (recall that a method is defined as the combination of a class and a selector, *e.g.,* WikiPage>>#document). Second, we instrument this method with one of the instrumentation methods added by BYTESURGEON to compiled methods, *e.g.,* #instrumentSends: or #instrumentInstVars:, to access all the specific operations in a method, *i.e.,* message sends or instance variables accesses, respectively. These instrumentation methods expect a block as single argument. In this block we have access to a block argument which denotes the current operation occurrence object. For a message send we get access to an instance of IRSend (this is part of the intermediate representation on which BYTESURGEON is based [11]).

Below is a short example showing how BYTESURGEON can be used to insert a simple piece of Smalltalk code into the method #document of class WikiPage:

```
(WikiPage>>#document) instrumentSends: [:send |
          send selector = #size ifTrue: [ send replace: '7']]
```

In this example we replace every send of the #size message occurring in the method #document of class WikiPage to simply return the constant 7. This example shows how to access different operations in a method (operation selection, *i.e.,* message sending) and how to select different operation occurrences (intra-operation selection; *i.e.,* message sends invoking #size) in a method.

During the instrumentation of a method the defined block is evaluated for every such operation in that method. To do intra-operation selection it is enough to specify a condition in the block, such as asking if the selector of an IRSend is of interest. Only if this condition is met the corresponding operation occurrence is adapted, either by replacing it or by inserting code before or after it. The code to be inserted is written as normal Smalltalk code directly in a string. In this string we can refer to dynamic information by using *meta variables*, such as <meta: *#receiver*> or <meta: *#arguments*> to reference respectively the receiver or the arguments of a method (more in [11]).

6.2   Structure of a Hook

In GEPPETTO, hooks are inserted in bytecode to provoke reification and delegation at runtime, where and when needed. The execution of a hook is a three-step process:

– Checking if the link is active for the currently-executing object;
– Reifying dynamic information and packing this information as specified by the call descriptor of the link;
– Performing the actual delegation to the metaobject, by sending the message specified in the call descriptor, with the corresponding reified information.

When a link has to be installed, GEPPETTO evaluates the static selectors (package, class, method, etc.) and then generates an appropriate string of Smalltalk code based on the specification of the call descriptor of the link. This string is then compiled and inserted by BYTESURGEON. For instance, for the cache link of Section 4.3, the generated Smalltalk code is:

```
(<meta: #link>  isActiveFor: self)
   ifTrue: [ <meta: #link>  metaobject cacheFor: <meta: #arg1> ].
```

First, the activation condition is checked. Note that the link itself is available as a meta variable for BYTESURGEON. If the link is active for the currently-executing object, then delegation occurs: the metaobject is retrieved from the link, and the cacheFor: message is sent with first argument as parameter.

The exact string generated depends on the call descriptor defining the message name, parameters, and passing mode. For instance if the passing mode is by array, it is necessary to first build up the array explicitly in the hook. The generated code also depends on the scope of the link (*e.g.,* if the link has object scope, then retrieving the metaobject requires passing the currently-executing object).

6.3   Hook Composition

If more than one hookset is installed in a given application, some hooks of different hooksets may conflict with each other, for instance if two hooksets affect the same message send of a given method. GEPPETTO is capable of detecting and also solving such a conflict automatically at runtime during the installation of every new link.

Detecting a hook conflict is a two-fold process: First, GEPPETTO determines for every link being installed, if another link also manipulates a given method, *i.e.,* if metalevel behavior is already installed in this method. GEPPETTO holds a global repository containing all installed links with a list of the affected classes and methods for each link. Querying this repository results in a collection of links affecting a given method. Second, GEPPETTO analyzes every instruction of a method to find out where exactly in the method body more than one link does install a hook. Concretely, the hook installer iterates over every instruction of such a method and tests for every conflicting link if it manipulates the current instruction. The following code illustrates this:

```
conflictingLinks do: [:eachLink |
    (method ir allInstructionsMatching: eachLink hookset operationSelector) do: [:instr |
        "this instruction is manipulated by the given link"
        self addLinkToRepository: eachLink forInstr: instr.
].
```

As soon as the hook installer has detected all the instructions conflicting with already installed links as described above, it solves the conflict by collecting first all the hooks manipulating a given instruction. Second, all these collected hooks are installed in sequence before, after or instead of the original instruction, depending on the control attribute specified in the link. The order in the sequence is determined by the installation time of the conflicting links, the first installed link will be installed first.

Note that there is not always a conflict when two links manipulate the same instruction of a method. If one link *e.g.,* executes metalevel behavior before the original instruction and the second one afterwards then these links do not conflict at this instruction. Hence the conflict detection algorithm has to take into account the controls of the links.

Finally, note that GEPPETTO adopts a simple automatic composition strategy; future work may include considering more advanced link composition strategies as supported by Reflex [22].

7   Evaluation

We now report on preliminary micro-benchmarks that validate the performance of GEPPETTO by comparing it with other reflective frameworks and architectures. We measure the slowdown of a fully reified message send over a non-reified message send. In Table 3 we compare the reflective systems Iguana/J [4], and MetaclassTalk [23] to GEPPETTO. The measurement for Iguana/J was taken from [4]. For MetaclassTalk and GEPPETTO, we performed the benchmarks on a Windows PC with an Intel Pentium 4 CPU 3.4 GHz and 3 GB RAM. The version of MetaclassTalk used was v0.3beta, GEPPETTO was running in Squeak 3.9. For a more detailed explanation and the source code of the benchmark, see [24].

We are comparing systems to GEPPETTO that do not provide partial reflection. As mentioned earlier, the real performance gain of partial reflection comes from the fact that we are able to exactly control what to reify and thus are able to minimize the reification costs. This benchmark does not cover this use but lets GEPPETTO reify every information about a message send to be comparable with the other systems. The benchmark will thus only give an impression of the worst case, *i.e.*, when GEPPETTO is doing full reification of a message send.

Table 3. Slowdowns of different reflective systems for the reification of message sends

System	slowdown factor
Geppetto	10.85
Iguana/J	24
MetaclassTalk	20

Because Iguana/J is using Java, we cannot do a direct time comparison with GEPPETTO. So we did such a comparison with MetaclassTalk, since both GEPPETTO and MetaclassTalk are running in the same environment. We implemented for the operations message sending and instance variable access the same metaobject protocol and the same behavior at the metalevel in both proposals to be able to compare the resulting execution time. The measured execution time includes the reification as well as the processing of the metalevel behavior. For message sending we reify the receiver, the selector and the arguments, for instance variable access the name of the variable and its value. Table 4 presents the results of this benchmark. For both operations, message send and instance variable access, we reified almost every possible information in GEPPETTO to get a reliable comparison with MetaclassTalk which does not support to control which information shall be reified, as described in Section 3.2. Hence GEPPETTO, supporting partial reification of information, will perform even better than the 2-to-3 times speedup against MetaclassTalk in cases where not every information about an operation occurrence is required.

To explain why GEPPETTO is so much faster than MetaclassTalk we have to understand that MetaclassTalk wraps every method (using MethodWrappers [17]) by default to allow message receive to be reified even when called from a class not under the control of MetaclassTalk. GEPPETTO on the other hand does not try to provide reified massage reception in this case, as we requested only a reification of message sending.

Table 4. Speedup of GEPPETTO over MetaclassTalk for reified message send and instance variable read access

	MetaclassTalk (ms)	GEPPETTO (ms)	Speedup
message send	108	46	2.3x
instance variable read	272	92	2.9x

These preliminary benchmarks tend to validate that the applied model for partial behavioral reflection is efficient compared to other models. Hence the combination of PBR and UBR is indeed fruitful and successful, because UPBR enables us to use unanticipated reflection in an efficient and effective manner.

8   Conclusion and Future Work

In this paper, we have motivated a particular form of computational reflection, called *unanticipated partial behavioral reflection*, which is particularly well-suited for unanticipated adaptation of real-world systems. Our proposal combines the dynamicity of unanticipated reflection, *i.e.,* reflection that does not require preparation of the code of any sort, and the selectivity, efficiency and flexibility of partial behavioral reflection. We have presented a system for unanticipated partial behavioral reflection in Squeak , called GEPPETTO, illustrated its use with a concrete example of a Seaside web application. Preliminary benchmarks validate the applicability of our proposal as an extension to the standard reflective abilities of Smalltalk.

In the future, we plan to work mainly in two directions: the first is to improve GEPPETTO itself, the second consists of using it in a number of projects. As far as improvements to GEPPETTO itself are concerned, we plan to explore advanced scoping for reifications (control-flow based, and more generally, contextual) to give the metaprogrammer even more means to control where and when reification should occur. Another track is to redesign the backend of GEPPETTO: we decided to use bytecode transformation as we could leverage the fast and easy to use BYTESURGEON framework. But bytecode is a very low-level representation means to trade performance with expressiveness. We plan to extend the Smalltalk structural meta model to provide a high-level model of sub-method structure and explore its use for GEPPETTO. We are currently working on a number of projects that could benefit from GEPPETTO. We have experimented with back-in-time debugging [25], but the prototype directly uses BYTESURGEON for now; we plan to explore how GEPPETTO can be used instead. Another interesting possibility is to use GEPPETTO as the basis for dynamic analysis [26].

Finally, we plan to explore dynamic aspects for Smalltalk with GEPPETTO. Because as argued in the body of work on versatile kernels for AOP [21,27], the flexible model of partial behavioral reflection on which both Reflex and GEP-PETTO are based is particularly well-suited to serve as an underlying infrastructure for AOP. This would then allow GEPPETTO to provide more elaborate AOP features than what the other known dynamic AOP systems for Smalltalk [28,29] do at present.

Acknowledgments. We acknowledge the financial support of the Swiss National Science Foundation for the projects "A Unified Approach to Composition and Extensibility" (SNF Project No. 200020-105091/1, Oct. 2004 - Sept. 2006) and "Analyzing, capturing and taming software change" (SNF Project No. 200020-113342, Oct. 2006 - Sept. 2008). É. Tanter is partially financed by the Millennium Nucleus Center for Web Research, Grant P04-067-F, Mideplan, Chile.

References

1. Gamma, E., Helm, R., Vlissides, J., Johnson, R.E.: Design patterns: Abstraction and reuse of object-oriented design. In Nierstrasz, O., ed.: Proceedings ECOOP '93. Volume 707 of LNCS., Kaiserslautern, Germany, Springer-Verlag (1993) 406–431
2. Rao, R.: Implementational reflection in Silica. In America, P., ed.: Proceedings ECOOP '91. Volume 512 of LNCS., Geneva, Switzerland, Springer-Verlag (1991) 251–267
3. Kiczales, G., Ashley, J., Rodriguez, L., Vahdat, A., Bobrow, D.G.: Metaobject protocols: Why we want them and what else they can do. In: Object-Oriented Programming: the CLOS Perspective. MIT Press (1993) 101–118
4. Redmond, B., Cahill, V.: Supporting unanticipated dynamic adaptation of application behaviour. In: Proceedings of European Conference on Object-Oriented Programming. Volume 2374., Springer-Verlag (2002) 205–230
5. Tarr, P.L., D'Hondt, M., Bergmans, L., Lopes, C.V.: Workshop on aspects and dimensions of concern: Requirements on, and challenge problems for, advanced separation of concerns. In Malenfant, J., Moisan, S., Moreira, A.M.D., eds.: ECOOP 2000 Workshops. Volume 1964 of LNCS., Springer (2000) 203–240
6. Smith, B.C.: Reflection and semantics in a procedural language. Technical Report TR-272, MIT, Cambridge, MA (1982)
7. Ferber, J.: Computational reflection in class-based object-oriented languages. In: Proceedings OOPSLA '89, ACM SIGPLAN Notices. Volume 24. (1989) 317–326
8. Maes, P.: Computational Reflection. PhD thesis, Laboratory for Artificial Intelligence, Vrije Universiteit Brussel, Brussels Belgium (1987)
9. McAffer, J.: Engineering the meta level. In Kiczales, G., ed.: Proceedings of the 1st International Conference on Metalevel Architectures and Reflection (Reflection 96), San Francisco, USA (1996)
10. Tanter, É., Noyé, J., Caromel, D., Cointe, P.: Partial behavioral reflection: Spatial and temporal selection of reification. In: Proceedings of OOPSLA '03, ACM SIGPLAN Notices. (2003) 27–46
11. Denker, M., Ducasse, S., Tanter, É.: Runtime bytecode transformation for Smalltalk. Journal of Computer Languages, Systems and Structures **32** (2006) 125–139

12. Ducasse, S., Lienhard, A., Renggli, L.: Seaside — a multiple control flow web application framework. In: Proceedings of ESUG International Smalltalk Conference 2004. (2004) 231–257
13. Goldberg, A., Robson, D.: Smalltalk 80: the Language and its Implementation. Addison Wesley, Reading, Mass. (1983)
14. Ingalls, D., Kaehler, T., Maloney, J., Wallace, S., Kay, A.: Back to the future: The story of Squeak, A practical Smalltalk written in itself. In: Proceedings OOPSLA '97, ACM SIGPLAN Notices, ACM Press (1997) 318–326
15. Rivard, F.: Smalltalk : a Reflective Language. In: Proceedings of REFLECTION '96. (1996) 21–38
16. Ducasse, S.: Evaluating message passing control techniques in Smalltalk. Journal of Object-Oriented Programming (JOOP) **12** (1999) 39–44
17. Brant, J., Foote, B., Johnson, R., Roberts, D.: Wrappers to the rescue. In: Proceedings European Conference on Object Oriented Programming (ECOOP 1998). Volume 1445 of LNCS., Springer-Verlag (1998) 396–417
18. Bouraqadi, N.: Un MOP Smalltalk pour l'étude de la composition et de la compatibilité des métaclasses. Application à la programmation par aspects (A Smalltalk MOP for the Study of Metaclass Composition and Compatibility. Application to Aspect-Oriented Programming - In French). Thèse de doctorat, Université de Nantes, Nantes, France (1999)
19. Bouraqadi, N.: Safe metaclass composition using mixin-based inheritance. Journal of Computer Languages, Systems and Structures **30** (2004) 49–61
20. Bouraqadi, N., Seriai, A., Leblanc, G.: Towards unified aspect-oriented programming. In: Proceedings of ESUG 2005 (13th International Smalltalk Conference). (2005)
21. Tanter, É., Noyé, J.: A versatile kernel for multi-language AOP. In: Proceedings of the 4th ACM SIGPLAN/SIGSOFT Conference on Generative Programming and Component Engineering (GPCE 2005). Volume 3676 of LNCS., Tallin, Estonia (2005)
22. Tanter, É.: Aspects of composition in the reflex aop kernel. In: Proceedings of the 5th International Symposium on Software Composition (SC 2006). LNCS, Vienna, Austria (2006) 99–114
23. Bouraqadi, N.: Concern oriented programming using reflection. In: Workshop on Advanced Separation of Concerns - OOPSLA 2000. (2000)
24. Röthlisberger, D.: Geppetto: Enhancing Smalltalk's reflective capabilities with unanticipated reflection. Master's thesis, University of Bern (2006)
25. Lewis, B.: Debugging backwards in time. In: Proceedings of the Fifth International Workshop on Automated Debugging (AADEBUG 2003). (2003)
26. Denker, M., Greevy, O., Lanza, M.: Higher abstractions for dynamic analysis. In: 2nd International Workshop on Program Comprehension through Dynamic Analysis (PCODA 2006). (2006) 32–38
27. Tanter, É., Noyé, J.: Motivation and requirements for a versatile AOP kernel. In: 1st European Interactive Workshop on Aspects in Software (EIWAS 2004), Berlin, Germany (2004)
28. Bergel, A.: FacetS: First class entities for an open dynamic AOP language. In: Proceedings of the Open and Dynamic Aspect Languages Workshop. (2006)
29. Hirschfeld, R.: AspectS – aspect-oriented programming with Squeak. In Aksit, M., Mezini, M., Unland, R., eds.: Objects, Components, Architectures, Services, and Applications for a Networked World. Number 2591 in LNCS, Springer (2003) 216–232

Stateful Traits

Alexandre Bergel[1], Stéphane Ducasse[2], Oscar Nierstrasz[3], and Roel Wuyts[4]

[1] DSG, Trinity College Dublin, Ireland
[2] Language and Software Evolution – LISTIC, Université de Savoie
[3] Software Composition Group, University of Bern
[4] Lab for Software Composition and Decomposition, Université Libre de Bruxelles

Abstract. Traits offer a fine-grained mechanism to compose classes from reusable components while avoiding problems of fragility brought by multiple inheritance and mixins. Traits as originally proposed are *stateless*, that is, they contain only methods, but no instance variables. State can only be accessed within traits by accessors, which become *required methods* of the trait. Although this approach works reasonably well in practice, it means that many traits, viewed as software components, are artificially *incomplete*, and classes that use such traits may contain significant amounts of boilerplate glue code. Although these limitations are largely mitigated by proper tool support, we seek a cleaner solution that supports *stateful traits*. The key difficulty is how to handle conflicts that arise when composed traits contribute instance variables whose names clash. We present a solution that is faithful to the guiding principle of stateless traits: *the client retains control of the composition*. Stateful traits consist of a minimal extension to stateless traits in which instance variables are purely local to the scope of a trait, unless they are explicitly made accessible by the composing client of a trait. Naming conflicts are avoided, and variables of disjoint traits can be explicitly merged by clients. We discuss and compare two implementation strategies, and briefly present a case study in which stateful traits have been used to refactor the trait-based version of the Smalltalk collection hierarchy.

1 Introduction

Traits are pure units of reuse consisting only of methods [SDNB03,DNS+06]. Traits can be composed to either form other traits or classes. They are recognized for their potential in supporting better composition and reuse, hence their integration in newer versions of languages such as Perl 6, Squeak [IKM+97], Scala [sca], Slate [Sla] and Fortress [for]. Although traits were originally designed for dynamically-typed languages, there has been considerable interest in applying traits to statically-typed languages as well [FR03, SD05, NDS06].

Traits make it possible for inheritance to be used to reflect conceptual hierarchy rather than for code reuse. Duplicated code can be factored out as traits, rather than being jimmied into a class hierarchy in awkward locations. At the same time, traits

W. De Meuter (Ed.): ISC 2006, LNCS 4406, pp. 66–90, 2007.

largely avoid the fragility problems introduced by approaches based on multiple inheritance and mixins, since traits are entirely divorced from the inheritance hierarchy.

In their original form, however, traits are *stateless*, *i.e.*, traits are purely groups of methods without any instance variables. Since traits not only provide methods, but may also *require* methods, the idiom introduced to deal with state was to access state only through accessors. The *client* of a trait is either a class or a composite trait that *uses* the trait to build up its implementation. A key principle behind traits is that *the client retains control of the composition*. The client, therefore, is responsible for providing the required methods, and resolving any possible conflicts. Required accessors would propagate to composite traits, and only the composing client class would be required to implement the missing accessors and the instance variables that they give access to. In practice, the accessors and instance variables could easily be generated by a tool, so the fact that traits were stateless posed only a minor nuisance.

Conceptually, however, the lack of state means that virtually all traits are *incomplete*, since just about any useful trait will require some accessors. Furthermore, the mechanism of required methods is abused to cover for the lack of state. As a consequence, the required interface of a trait is cluttered with noise that impedes the understanding and consequently the reuse of a trait. Even if the missing state and accessors can be generated, many clients will consist of "shell classes" — classes that do nothing but compose traits with boilerplate glue code. Furthermore, if the required accessors are made public (as is the case in the Smalltalk implementation), encapsulation is unnecessarily violated in the client classes. Finally, if a trait is ever modified to include additional state, new required accessors will be propagated to all client traits and classes, thus introducing a form of fragility that traits were intended to avoid!

This paper describes *stateful traits*, an extension of stateless traits in which a single variable access operator is introduced to give clients of traits control over the visibility of instance variables. The approach is faithful to the guiding principle of stateless traits in which the client of a trait has full control over the composition. It is this principle that is the key to avoiding fragility in the face of change, since no implicit conflict resolution rules come into play when a trait is modified.

In a nutshell, instance variables are private to a trait. The client can decide, however, at composition time to *access* instance variables offered by a used trait, or to *merge* variables offered by multiple traits. In this paper we present an analysis of the limitations of stateless traits and we present our approach to achieving stateful traits. We describe and compare two implementation strategies, and we briefly describe our experience with an illustrative case study.

The structure of this paper is as follows: First we review stateless traits [SDNB03, DNS+06]. In Section 3 we discuss the limitations of stateless traits. In Section 4 we introduce stateful traits, which support the introduction of state in traits. Section 5 outlines some details of the implementation of stateful traits. In Section 6 we present a small case study in which we compare the results of refactoring the Smalltalk collections hierarchy with both stateless and stateful traits. In Section 7 we discuss some of the broader consequences of the design of stateful traits. Section 8 discusses related work. Section 9 concludes the paper.

2   Stateless Traits

2.1   Reusable Groups of Methods

Stateless traits are sets of methods that serve as the behavioural building block of classes and primitive units of code reuse [DNS⁺06]. In addition to offering behaviour, traits also *require methods, i.e.,* methods that are needed so that trait behaviour is fulfilled. Traits do not define state, instead they require accessor methods.

In Figure 1, the trait TSyncReadWrite provides the methods syncRead, syncWrite and hash. It requires the methods read and write, and the two accessor methods lock and lock:. We use an extension to UML to represent traits (the right column lists required methods while the left one lists the provided methods).

2.2   Composing Classes from Mixins

The following equation depicts how a class is built with traits:

$$class = superclass + state + trait\ composition + glue\ code$$

A class is specified from a superclass, state definition, a set of traits, and some *glue methods*. Glue methods are defined in the class and they connect the traits together; *i.e.,* they implement required trait methods (often for accessing state), they adapt provided trait methods, and they resolve method conflicts.

In Figure 1, the class SyncStream defines the field lock and the glue methods lock, lock:, isBusy and hash. The other required methods of TSyncReadWrite, read and write, are also provided since the class SyncStream uses another trait TStream which provides them.

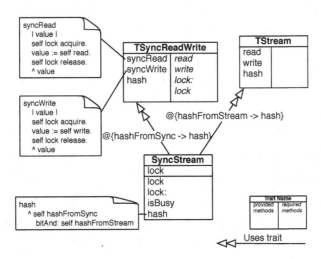

Fig. 1. The class SyncStream is composed of the two traits TSyncReadWrite and TStream

Trait composition respects the following three rules:

- Methods defined in the class take precedence over trait methods. This allows the glue methods defined in a class to override methods with the same name provided by the used traits.
- Flattening property. A non-overridden method in a trait has the same semantics as if it were implemented directly in the class using the trait.
- Composition order is irrelevant. All the traits have the same precedence, and hence conflicting trait methods must be explicitly disambiguated.

With this approach, classes retain their primary role as generators of instances, whereas traits are purely behavioural units of reuse. As with mixins, classes are organized in a single inheritance hierarchy, thus avoiding the key problems of multiple inheritance, but the incremental extensions that classes introduce to their superclasses are specified using one or more traits. In contrast to mixins, several traits can be applied to a class in a single operation: trait composition is unordered. Instead of the trait composition resulting implicitly from the order in which traits are composed (as is the case with mixins), it is fully under the control of the composing class.

2.3 Conflict Resolution

While composing traits, method conflicts may arise. A *conflict* arises if we combine two or more traits that provide identically named methods that do not originate from the same trait. Conflicts are resolved by implementing a method at the level of the class that *overrides* the conflicting methods, or by *excluding* a method from all but one trait. In addition traits allow method *aliasing*; this makes it possible for the programmer to introduce an additional name for a method provided by a trait. The new name is used to obtain access to a method that would otherwise be unreachable because it has been overridden [DNS+06].

In Figure 1, methods in TSyncReadWrite and in TStream are used by Sync-Stream. The trait composition associated to SyncStream is:

TSyncReadWrite@{hashFromSync→hash} + TStream@{hashFromStream→hash}

This means that SyncStream is composed of (i) the trait TSyncReadWrite for which the method hash is aliased to hashFromSync and (ii) the trait TStream for which the method hash is aliased to hashFromStream.

2.4 Method Composition Operators

The semantics of traits composition is based on four operators: sum, overriding, exclusion and aliasing [DNS+06].

The *sum* trait TSyncReadWrite + TStream contains all of the non-conflicting methods of TSyncReadWrite and TStream. If there is a method conflict, that is, if TSyncRead-Write and TStream both define a method with the same name, then in TSyncReadWrite + TStream that name is bound to a distinguished conflict method. The + operator is associative and commutative.

The *overriding* operator constructs a new composition trait by extending an existing trait composition with some explicit local definitions. For instance, SyncStream overrides the method hash obtained from its trait composition. This can also be done with methods, as we will discuss in more detail later.

A trait can be constructed by *excluding* methods from an existing trait using the exclusion operator −. Thus, for instance, TStream − {read, write} has a single method hash. Exclusion is used to avoid conflicts, or if one needs to reuse a trait that is "too big" for one's application.

The *method aliasing* operator @ creates a new trait by providing an additional name for an existing method. For example, if TStream is a trait that defines read, write and hash, then TStream @ {hashFromStream →hash} is a trait that defines read, write, hash and hashFromStream. The additional method hashFromStream has the same body as the method hash. Aliases are used to make conflicting methods available under another name, perhaps to meet the requirements of some other trait, or to avoid overriding. Note that because the body of the aliased method is not changed in any way, so an alias to a recursive method is not recursive.

3   Limitations of Stateless Traits

Traits support the reuse of coherent groups of methods by otherwise independent classes [DNS[+]06]. Traits can be composed out of other traits. As a consequence they serve well as a medium for structuring code. Unfortunately stateless traits necessarily encode dependency on state in terms of required methods (*i.e.*, accessors). In essence, traits are necessarily *incomplete* since virtually any useful trait will be forced to define required accessors. This means that the composing class must define the missing instance variables and accessors.

The incompleteness of traits results in a number of annoying limitations, namely: (i) trait reusability is impacted because the required interface is typically cluttered with uninteresting required accessors, (ii) client classes are forced to implement boilerplate glue code, (iii) the introduction of new state in a trait propagates required accessors to all client classes, and (iv) public accessors break encapsulation of the client class.

Although these annoyances can be largely addressed by proper tool support, they disturb the appeal of traits as a clean, lightweight mechanism for composing classes from reusable components. A proper understanding of these limitations is a prerequisite to entertaining any proposal for a more general approach.

3.1   Limited Reusability

The fact that a stateless trait is forced to encode state in terms of required accessors means that it cannot be composed "off-the-shelf" without some additional action. Virtually every useful trait is incomplete, even though the missing part can be trivially fulfilled.

What's worse, however, is the fact that the required interface of a trait is cluttered with dependencies on uninteresting required accessors, rather than focussing attention on the non-trivial hook methods that clients must implement.

Although this problem can be partially alleviated with proper tool support that distinguishes the uninteresting required accessors from the other required methods, the fact

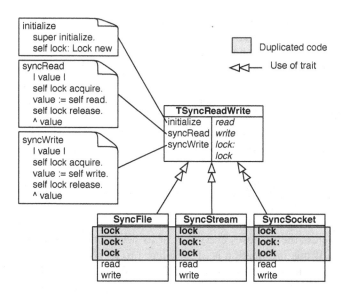

Fig. 2. The lock variable, the lock and lock: methods are duplicated among trait TSyncRead-Write users

remains that traits with required accessors can never be reused off-the-shelf without additional action by the ultimate client class.

3.2 Boilerplate Glue Code

The necessary additional client action consists essentially in the generation of boilerplate glue code to inject the missing instance variables, accessors and initialization code. Clearly this boilerplate code must be generated for each and every client class. In the most straightforward approach, this will lead to the kind of duplicated code that traits were intended to avoid.

Figure 2 illustrates such a situation where the trait TSyncReadWrite needs to access a lock. This lock variable, the lock accessor and the lock: mutator have to be duplicated in SyncFile, SyncStream and SyncSocket.

Once again, to avoid this situation, tool support would be required (i) to automatically generate the required instance variables and accessors, and (ii) to generate the code in such a way as to avoid actual duplication.

Another unpleasant side effect of the need for boilerplate glue code is the emergence of "shell classes" consisting of nothing but glue code. In the Smalltalk hierarchy refactored using stateless traits [BSD03], we note that 24% (7 out of 29) of the classes in the hierarchy refactored with traits are pure shell classes.

3.3 Propagation of Required Accessors

If a trait implementation evolves and requires new variables, it may impact all the classes that use it, even if the interface remains untouched. For instance, if the implementation of the trait TSyncReadWrite evolves and requires a new variable numberWaiting intended to give the number of clients waiting for the lock, then all the classes using this trait are impacted, even though the public interface does not change.

Required accessors are propagated and accumulated from trait to trait, therefore when a class is composed of deeply composed traits, a large number of accessors may need to be resolved. When a new state dependency is introduced in a deeply nested trait, required accessors can be propagated to a large number of client classes. Again, proper tool support can largely mitigate the consequences of such changes, but a more satisfactory solution would be welcome.

3.4   Violation of Encapsulation

Stateless traits violate encapsulation in two ways. First of all, stateless traits unnecessarily expose information about their internal representation, thus muddying their interface. A stateless trait exposes every part of its needed representation as a required accessor, even if this information is of no interest to its clients. Encapsulation would be better served if traits resembled more closely abstract classes, where only abstract methods are explicitly declared as being the responsibility of the client subclass. By the same token, a client class using a trait should only see those required methods that are truly its responsibility to implement, and no others.

The second violation is about visibility. In Smalltalk, instance variables are always private. Access can be granted to other objects by providing public accessors. But if traits require accessors, then classes using these traits *must* provide public accessors to the missing state, even if this is not desired.

In principle, this problem could be somewhat mitigated in Java-like languages by including visibility modifiers for stateless traits in Java-like languages. A trait could then require a private or protected accessor for missing state. The client class could then supply these accessors without violating encapsulation (and optionally relaxing the required modifier). This solution, however, would not solve the problem for Smalltalk-like languages in which all methods are public, and may only be marked as "private" by convention (*i.e.*, by placing such methods in a category named "private").

4   Stateful Traits: Reconciling Traits and State

We now present stateful traits as our solution to the limitations of stateless traits. Although it may seem that adding instance variables to traits would represent a trivial extension, in fact there are a number of issues that need to be resolved. Briefly, our solution addresses the following concerns:

- Stateless traits should be a special case of stateful traits. The original semantics of stateless traits (and the advantages of that solution) should not be impacted.
- Any extension should be syntactically and semantically minimal. We seek a simple solution.
- We should address the limitations listed in Section 3. In particular, it should be possible to express complete traits. Only methods that are conceptually the responsibility of client classes should be listed as required methods.

– The solution should offer sensible default semantics for trait usage, thus enabling black-box usage.
– Consistent with the guiding principle of stateless traits, the client class should retain control over the composition, in particular over the policy for resolving conflicts. A degree of white-box usage is therefore also supported, where needed.
– As with stateless traits, we seek to avoid fragility with respect to change. Changes to the representation of a trait should normally not affect its clients.
– The solution should be largely language independent. We do not depend on obscure or exotic language features, so the approach should easily apply to most object-oriented languages.

The solution we present extends traits to possibly include instance variables. In a nutshell, there are three aspects to our approach:

1. Instance variables are, by default, *private* to the scope of the trait that defines them.
2. The client of a trait, *i.e.*, a class or a composite trait, may *access* selected variables of that trait, mapping those variables to possibly new names. The new names are private to the scope of the client.
3. The client of a composite trait may *merge* variables of the traits it uses by mapping them to a common name. The new name is private to the scope of the client.

In the following subsections we provide details of the stateful traits model.

4.1 Stateful Trait Definition

A stateful trait extends a stateless trait by including private instance variables. A stateful trait therefore consists of a group of public methods and private instance variables, and possibly a specification of some additional required methods to be implemented by clients.

Methods. Methods defined in a trait are visible to any other trait with which it is composed. Because methods are public, conflicts may occur when traits are composed. Method conflicts for stateful traits are resolved in the same way as with stateless traits.
Variables. By default, variables are private to the trait that defines them. Because variables are private, conflicts between variables cannot occur when traits are composed. If, for example, traits T1 and T2 each define a variable x, then the composition of T1 + T2 does *not* yield a variable conflict. Variables are only visible to the trait that defines them, unless access is widened by the composing client trait or class with the @@ variable access operator.

Figure 3 shows how the situation presented in Figure 1 is reimplemented using stateful traits. The class SyncStream is composed of the traits TStream and TSyncReadWrite. The trait TSyncReadWrite defines the variable lock, three methods syncRead, syncWrite and hash, and requires methods read and write.

Note that, in order to include state in traits, we must extend the mechanism for defining traits. In the Smalltalk implementation, this is achieved by extending the message

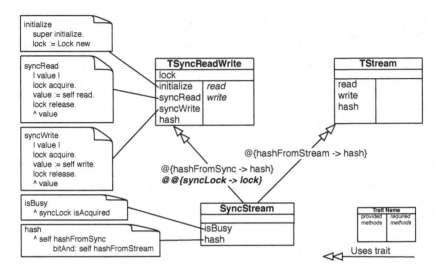

Fig. 3. The class SyncStream is composed of the stateful traits TStream and TSyncReadWrite

sent to the Trait class with a new keyword argument to represent the used instance variables. For instance, we can now define the TSyncReadWrite trait as follows:

```
Trait named: #TSyncReadWrite
    uses: {}
    instVarNames: 'lock'
```

The trait TSyncReadWrite is not composed of any other traits and it defines a variable lock. The uses: clause specifies the trait composition (empty in this case), and instVarNames: lists the variables defined in the trait (*i.e.*, the variable, lock). The interface for defining a class as composition of traits is the same as with stateless traits. The only difference is that the trait composition expression supports an additional operator (@@) for granting access to variables of the used traits. Here we see how SyncStream is composed from the traits TSyncReadWrite and TStream:

```
Object subclass: #SyncStream
    uses: TSyncReadWrite @ {#hashFromSync →#hash}
          @@ {syncLock →lock}
        + TStream @ {#hashFromStream →#hash}
    instVarNames: "
    ....
```

In this example, access is granted to the lock variable of the TSyncReadWrite trait under the new name syncLock. As we shall now see, the @@ operator provides a fine degree of control over the visibility of trait variables.

4.2   Variable Access

By default, a variable is private to the trait that defines it. However, the variable access operator (@@) allows variables to be *accessed* from clients under a possibly new name, and possibly *merged* with other variables.

If T is a trait that defines a (private) instance variable x, then T@@{y →x} represents a new trait in which the variable x can be accessed from its client scope under the name y. x and y represent the same variable, but the name x is restricted to the scope of t whereas the name y is visible to the enclosing client scope (*i.e.*, the composing classscope). For instance, in the following composition:

$$\text{TSyncReadWrite} @ \{\text{hashFromSync} \rightarrow \text{hash}\} @ @ \{\text{syncLock} \rightarrow \text{lock}\}$$

the variable lock defined in TSyncReadWrite is accessible to the class SyncStream using that trait under the name syncLock. (Note that renaming is often needed to distinguish similarly named variables coming from different used traits.)

In a trait variable composition, three situations can arise: (i) variables remain private (*i.e.*, the variable access operator is not used), (ii) access to a private variable is granted, and (iii) variables are merged.

Keeping variables private. By default, instance variables are private to their trait. If the scope of variables is not broadened at composition time using the variable access operator, conflicts do not occur and the traits do not share state. Figure 4 shows a case where T1 and T2 are composed without variable access being broadened. Each of these two traits defines a variable x. In addition they each define accessor methods. C also defines a variable x and two methods getX and setX:. T1, T2 and C each have their own variable x as shown in Figure 4.

The trait composition of C is: T1 + T2. Note that if methods would conflict we would use the default trait strategy to resolve them by locally redefining them in C and that method aliasing could be used to access the overridden methods.

This form of composition is close to the module composition approach proposed in Jigsaw [Bra92] and supports a black-box reuse scenario.

Granting variable access. Figure 5 shows how the client class C gains access to the private x variables of traits T1 and T2 by using the variable access operator @@. Because two variables cannot have the same name within a given scope, these variables have to be renamed. The variable x from T1 is accessible as xFromT1 and x from T2 is accessible as xFromT2. C also defines a method sum that returns the value xFromT1 + xFromT2. The trait composition of C is:

T1 @@ {xFromT1 →x}
+ T2 @@ {xFromT2 →x}

C can therefore build functionality on top of the traits that it uses, without exposing any details to the outside. Note that methods in the trait continue to use the 'internal' name of the variable as defined in the trait. The name given in the variable access operator @@ is only to be used in the client classes. This is similar to the method aliasing operator @.

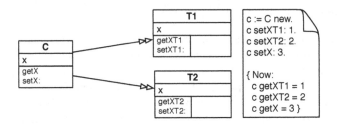

Fig. 4. Keeping variables private: while composed, variables are kept separate. Traits T1, T2 and C have their own variable x.

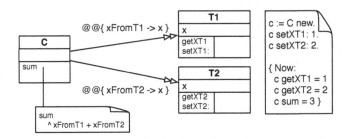

Fig. 5. Granting access to variables: x of T1 and T2 are given access in C

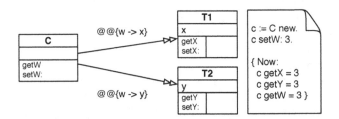

Fig. 6. Merging variables: variables x and y are merged in C under the name w

Merging variables. Variables from several traits can be merged when they are composed by using the variable access operator to map multiple variables to a *common name* within the client scope. This is illustrated in Figure 6.

Both T1 and T2 give access to their instance variables x and y under the name w. This means that w is shared between all three traits. This is the reason why sending getX, getY, or getW to an instance of a class implementing C returns the same result, 3. The trait composition of C is:

T1 @ @ {w →x} + T2 @ @ {w →y}

Note that merging is *fully* under the control of the client class or trait. There can be no accidental name capture since visibility of instance variables is never propagated to an enclosing scope. Variable name conflicts cannot arise, since variables are private to traits unless they are explicitly accessed by clients, and variables are merged when they are mapped to common names.

The reader might well ask, what happens if the client also defines an instance variable whose name happens to match the name under which a used trait's variable is accessed? Suppose, for example, that C in Figure 6 attempts to additionally define an instance variable called w. We consider this to be an error. This situation cannot possibly arise as a side effect of changing the definition of a used trait since the client has full control over the names of instance variables accessible within its scope. As a consequence this cannot be a case of accidental name capture, and can only be interpreted as an error.

4.3   Requirements Revisited

Let us briefly reconsider our requirements. First, stateful traits do not change the semantics of stateless traits. Stateless traits are purely a special case of stateful traits. Syntactically and semantically, stateful traits represent only a minor extension of stateless traits.

Stateful traits address the issues raised in Section 3. In particular, (i) there is no longer a need to clutter trait interfaces with required accessors, (ii) clients no longer need to provide boilerplate instance variables and accessors, (iii) the introduction of state in traits remains private to that trait, and (iv) no public accessors need be introduced in client classes. As a consequence, it is possible to define "complete" traits that require no methods, even though they make use of state.

The default semantics of stateful traits enables black-box usage since no representation is exposed, and instance variables by default cannot clash with those of the client or of other used traits. Nevertheless, the client retains control of the composition, and can gain access to the instance variables of used traits. In particular, the client may merge variables of traits, if this is desired.

Since the client retains full control of the composition, changes to the definition of a trait cannot propagate beyond its direct clients. There can be no implicit side effects.

Finally, the approach is largely language-independent. In particular, there are no assumptions that the host language provide either access modifiers for instance variables or exotic scoping mechanisms.

5   Implementation

We have implemented a prototype of stateful traits as an extension of our Smalltalk-based implementation of stateless traits.[1]

As with stateless traits, method composition and reuse for stateful traits do not incur any overhead since method pointers are shared between method dictionaries of different traits and classes. This takes advantage of the fact that methods are looked up by name in the dictionary rather than accessed by index and offset, as is done to access state in most object-oriented programming languages. However, by adding state to traits, we have to find a solution to the fact that the access to instance variables cannot be linear (*i.e.*, based on offsets) since the same trait methods can be applied to different objects [BGG+02]. A linear structure for state representation cannot be always obtained

---

[1] See www.iam.unibe.ch/~scg/Research/Traits

from a composition graph. This is a common problem of languages that support multiple inheritance. We evaluated two implementations: copy-down and changing object internal representation. The following section illustrates the problem.

5.1   The Classical Problem of State Linearization

As pointed out by Bracha [Bra92, Chapter 7], in implementations of single inheritance languages such as Modula-3 [CDG$^+$92], and more recently in the Jikes Research Virtual Machine [Jik], the notion of virtual functions is supported by associating to each class a table whose entries are the addresses of the methods defined for instances of that class. Each instance of a class contains a reference to the class method table. It is through this reference that the appropriate method to be invoked on an instance is located. Under multiple inheritance, this technique must be modified, since the superclasses of a class no longer share a common prefix.

Since a stateful trait may have a private state, and may be used in multiple contexts, it is not possible to have a static and linear instance variable offset list shared by all the methods of the trait and its users.

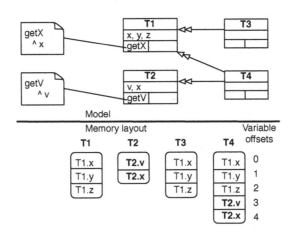

Fig. 7. Problem of combining multiple traits: variable's offset is not preserved

The top half of Figure 7 shows a trait T3 using T1 and a trait T4 using T1 and T2. T1 defines 3 variables x, y, z and T2 defines 2 variables v, x. The bottom part shows a possible corresponding representation in memory that uses offsets. Assuming that we start the indexing at zero, T2.v has zero for index, and T2.x has one. However, in T4 the same two variables might have indexes three and four.[2] So static indexes used in methods from T1 or T2 are no longer valid. Note that this problem occurs regardless of the composition of trait T4 out of traits T1 and T2 (whether it needs access to variables, whether or not it merges variable x, ...). The problem is due to the linear representation of variables in the underlying object model.

---

[2] We assume that the slots of T2 are added after the ones of T1. In the opposite case the argument holds for the variables of T1.

5.2 Three Approaches to State Linearization

Three different approaches are available to represent non linear state. C++ uses intra-object pointers [SG99]. Strongtalk [BGG+02] uses a *copy-down* technique that duplicates methods that need to access variable with different offset. A third approach, as done in Python [Pyt] for example, is to keep variables in a dictionary and look them up, similar to what is done for methods.

We implemented the last two approaches for Smalltalk so that we could compare them for our prototype implementation. We did not implement C++'s solution because it would require significant effort to change the object representation to be compatible.

5.3 Virtual Base Pointers in C++

In C++ [SE90], an instance of a class C is represented by concatenating the representations of superclasses of C. Such instance is therefore composed of *subobjects*, where each *subobject* corresponds to a particular *superclass*. Each subobject has its own pointer to a suitable method table. In this case, the representation of a class is not a prefix of the representations of all of its subclasses.

Each subobject begins at a different offset from the beginning of the complete C object. These offsets, called *virtual base pointers* [SG99], can be computed statically. This technique was pioneered by Krogdahl [Kro85, Bra92].

For instance, let's consider the situation in C++ illustrated in Figure 8. The upper part of the figure shows a classical diamond diagram using virtual inheritance (*i.e.*, B and C inherit virtually A, therefore the w variable is shared between B and C). The

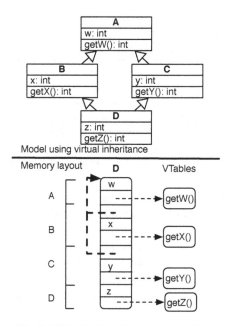

Fig. 8. Multiple virtual inheritance in C++

lower part shows the memory layout of an instance of D. This instance is composed of 4 "sub-parts" corresponding to the superclasses A, B, C and D. Note that C's part, instead of assuming that the state it inherits from A lies immediately "above" its own state, accesses the inherited state via the virtual base pointer. In this way the B and C parts of the D instance can share the same common state from A.

We did not attempt to implement this strategy in our Smalltalk prototype, as it would have required a deep modification to the Smalltalk VM. Since Smalltalk supports only single inheritance, object layout is fundamentally simpler. Accommodating virtual base pointers in the layout of an object would also entail changes to the method lookup algorithm.

5.4   Object State as a Dictionary

An alternative implementation approach is to introduce instance variable accesses based on names and not on offsets. The variable layout has the semantics of a hash table, rather than that of an array. For a given variable, its offset is not constant anymore as shown by Figure 9. The state of an object is implemented by a hash table in which multiple keys may map to the same value. For instance, variable y of T1 and variable v of T2 are merged in T4. Therefore, an instance of T4 has two variables (keys), T1.y and T2.v, that actually point to the same value.

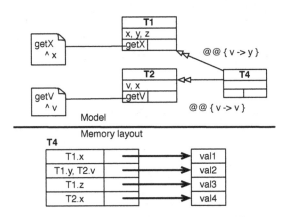

Fig. 9. Structure of objects is similar to a hash table with multiple keys for a same entry

In Python [Pyt] the state of an object is represented by a dictionary. An expression such as self.name = value is translated into self._dict_[name] = value, where _dict_ is a primitive to access the dictionary of an object. A variable is declared and defined simply by being used in Python. For instance, affecting a value to an non-existing variable has the effect to create a new variable. Representing the state of an object with a dictionary is a way to deal with the linearization problem of multiple inheritance.

5.5   Copy Down Methods

Strongtalk [BGG+02] is a high performance Smalltalk with a mixin-aware virtual machine. A mixin contains description of its instance variables and class variables, and a method dictionary where all the code is initially stored. One of the problems when sharing code among mixin application is that the physical layout of instances varies between mixin applications. This problem is addressed by the *copy down* mechanism: (i) Methods that do not access instance variables or **super** are shared in the mixin. (ii) Methods that access instance variables may have to be copied if the variable layout differs from that of other users of the mixin.

The copy down mechanism favors execution speed over memory consumption. There is no extra overhead to access variables. Variables are linearly ordered, and methods that access them are duplicated and adjusted with proper offset access. Moreover, in Strongtalk, only accessors are allowed to touch instance variables directly at the byte code level. The space overhead of copy-down is therefore minimal. Effective inlining by the VM takes care of the rest, except for accessors which impose no space overhead.

The dictionary-based approach has the advantage that it more directly reflects the semantics of stateful traits, and is therefore attractive for a prototype implementation. Practical performance could however become problematic, even with optimized dictionary implementations like in Python [Pyt]. The copy-down approach, however, is clearly the better approach for a fast implementation. Therefore we decided to adopt it in our implementation of stateful traits in Squeak Smalltalk.

5.6 Benchmarks

As mentioned in the previous section, we adopted the copy-down technique for our stateful traits implementation. In this section we compare the performance of our stateful traits prototype implementation with that of both regular Squeak without traits and that of the stateless traits implementation. We measured the performance of the following two case studies:

- the SyncStream example introduced in the beginning of the paper. The experiment consisted of writing and reading large objects in a stream 1000 times. This example was chosen to evaluate whether state is accessed efficiently.
- a link checker application that parses HTML pages to check whether URLs on a webpage are reachable or not. This entails parsing large HTML files into a tree representation and running visitors over these trees. This case study was chosen in order to have a more balanced example that consists of accessing methods as well as state.

For both case studies we compared the stateful implementation with the stateless traits implementation and with reular Squeak. The results are shown in Table 1.

Table 1. Execution times of two cases for three implementations: without traits, with stateless traits and with stateful traits (times in milliseconds)

	Without traits	Stateless traits	Stateful traits
SyncStream	13912	13913	13912
LinkChecker	2564	2563	2564

As can be seen from the table, no overhead is introduced by accessing instance variables defined in traits and used in clients. This was to be expected: the access is still offset-based and almost no differences can be noticed. Regarding overall execution speed, we see that there is essentially no difference between the three implementations. This result is consistent with previous experience using traits, and was to be expected since we did not change the parts of the implementation dealing with methods.

6   Refactoring the Smalltalk Collection Hierarchy

We have carried out a case study in which we used stateful traits to refactor the Smalltalk collection hierarchy. We have previously used stateless traits to refactor the same hierarchy [BSD03], and we now compare the results of the two refactorings. The stateless trait-based Smalltalk collection hierarchy consists of 29 classes which are built from a total of 52 traits. Among these 29 classes there are numerous classes, which we call *shell* classes, that only declare variables and define their associated accessors. Seven classes of the 29 classes (24%) are shell classes (SkipList, PluggableSet, LinkedList, OrderedCollection, Heap, Text and Dictionary).

The refactoring with stateful traits results in a redistribution of the variables defined (in classes) to the traits that effectively need and use them. Another consequence is the decrease of number of required methods and a better encapsulation of the traits behaviour and internal representation.

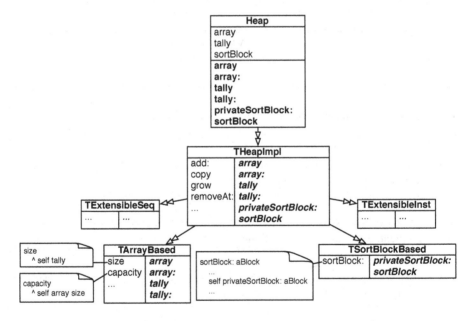

Fig. 10. Fragment of the stateless trait Smalltalk collection hierarchy. The class Heap defines variables used by TArrayBased and TSortBlockBased.

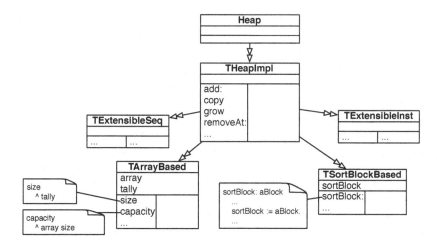

Fig. 11. Refactoring of the class Heap with stateful traits but keeping the trait THeapImpl

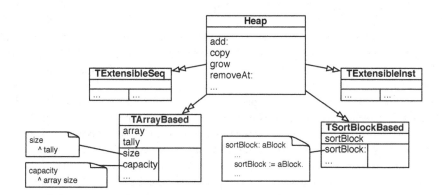

Fig. 12. Refactoring of the class Heap with stateful traits removing the trait THeapImpl

Figure 10 shows a typical case arising with stateless traits where the class Heap must define 3 variables (array, tally, and sortBlock). The behaviour of this class is limited to the initialization of objects and providing accessors for each of these variables. It uses the trait THeapImpl, which requires all these accessors. These requirements are necessary for THeapImpl since it is composed of TArrayBased and TSortBlockBased which require such state. These two traits need access to the state defined in Heap.

Figure 11 shows how Heap is refactored to use stateful traits. All variables have been moved to the places where they were needed, leading to the result that Heap becomes empty. The variables previously defined in Heap are rather defined in the traits that effectively require them. TArrayBased defines two variables array and tally, therefore it does not need to specify any accessors as required methods. It is the same situation with TSortBlockBased and the variable sortBlock.

If we are sure that THeapImpl is not used by any other class or trait, then we can further simplify this new composition by moving the implementation of the trait

THeapImpl to Heap and eliminating THeapImpl. Figure 12 shows the resulting hierarchy. The class Heap defines methods like add: and copy.

Refactoring the Smalltalk class hierarchy using stateful traits yields multiple benefits:

- *Encapsulation is preserved:* Internal representation is not unnecessarily revealed to client classes.
- *Fewer method definitions:* Unnecessary variable accessors are avoided. Accessors that were defined in Heap are removed.
- *Fewer method requirements:* Since variables are defined in the traits that used them, we avoid specifying required accessors. Variable accessors for THeapImpl, TArrayBased, and TSortBlockBased are not required anymore. There is no propagation of required methods due to state usage.

7   Discussion

7.1   Flattening Property

In the original stateless trait model [DNS+06], trait composition respects the *flattening property*, which states that a non-overridden method in a trait has the same semantics as if it were implemented directly in the class. This implies that traits can be inlined to give an equivalent class definition that does not use traits. It is natural to ask whether such an important property is preserved with stateful traits. In short, the answer is yes, though trait variables may have to be alpha-renamed to avoid name clashes.

In order to preserve the flattening property with stateful traits, we must ensure that instance variables introduced by traits remain private to the scope of that trait's methods, even when their scope is broadened to that of the composing class. This can be done in a variety of ways, depending on the scoping mechanisms provided by the host language. Semantically, however, the simplest approach is to alpha-rename the private instance variables of the trait to names that are unique in the client's scope. Technically, this could be achieved by the common technique of *name-mangling, i.e.*, by prepending the trait's name to the variable's name when inserting it in the client's scope. Renaming and merging are also consistent with flattening, since variables can simply be renamed or merged in the client's scope.

7.2   Limiting Change Impact

Any approach to composing software is bound to be fragile with respect to certain kinds of change: if a feature that is used by several clients changes, the change will affect the clients. Extending a trait so that it provides additional methods may well affect clients by introducing new conflicts. However, the design of trait composition based on explicit resolution ensures that such changes cannot lead to implicit and unexpected changes in the behaviour of direct or indirect clients. A direct client can generally resolve a conflict without changing or introducing any other traits, so no ripple effect will occur [DNS+06].

In stateful traits adding a variable to a trait does not affect clients because variables are private. Removing or renaming a variable may require its direct clients to be adapted only if this variable is explicitly accessed by these clients. However, once the direct clients have been adapted, no ripple effect can occur in indirect clients. By avoiding required method propagation, stateful traits limit the effect of changes.

7.3   About Variable Access

By default a trait variable is private, thereby enforcing black-box reuse. At the same time we offer an operator enabling the direct client to access the private variables of the trait. This may appear to be a violation of encapsulation [Sny86]. However this approach is consistent with our vision that traits serve as building blocks for composing classes, whether in a black-box or a white-box fashion. Furthermore it is consistent with the principle that the client of a trait is in control of the composition. It is precisely this fact that ensures that the effects of changes do not propagate to remote corners of the class hierarchy.

8   Related Work

We briefly review some of the numerous research activities that are relevant to stateful traits.

Self. The prototype based language Self [US87] does not have a notion of class. Conceptually, each object defines its own format, methods, and delegation relations. Objects are derived from other objects by cloning and modification. Objects can have one or more parent objects; messages that are not found in the object are looked for and delegated to a parent object. Self is based around the notion of slots, which unifies methods and instance variables.

Self uses trait objects to factor out common features [UCCH91]. Nothing prevents a trait object from also containing state. Similar to the notion of traits presented here, these trait objects are essentially groups of methods. But unlike our traits, Self's trait objects do not support specific composition operators; instead, they are used as ordinary parent objects.

Interfaces with default implementation. Mohnen [Moh02] proposed an extension of Java in which interfaces can be equipped with a set of default implementations of methods. As such, classes that implement such an interface can explicitly state that they want to use the default implementation offered by that interface (if any). If more than one interface mentions the same method, a method body must be provided. Conflicts are flagged automatically, but require the developer to resolve them manually. State cannot be associated with the interfaces. Scala [sca] also supports traits *i.e.*, partially defined interfaces. While the composition of traits in Scala does not follow exactly the one in stateless traits, traits in Scala cannot define state.

Mixins. Mixins [BC90] use the ordinary single inheritance operator to extend various parent classes with a bundled set of features. Although this inheritance operator is well-suited for deriving new classes from existing ones, it is not necessarily appropriate for composing reusable building blocks. Specifically, because mixin composition is implemented using single inheritance, mixins are composed linearly. This gives rise to several problems. First, a suitable total ordering of features may be difficult to find, or may not even exist. Second,"glue code" that exploits or adapts the linear composition may be dispersed throughout the class hierarchy. Third, the resulting class hierarchies are often fragile with respect to change, so that conceptually simple changes may impact many parts of the hierarchy [DNS⁺06].

Eiffel. Eiffel [Mey92] is a pure object-oriented language that supports multiple inheritance. Features, *i.e.*, method or instance variables, may be multiply inherited along different paths. Eiffel provides the programmer mechanisms that offer a fine degree of control over whether such features are shared or replicated. In particular, features may be *renamed* by the inheriting class. It is also possible to *select* a particular feature in case of naming conflicts. Selecting a feature means that from the context of the composing subclass, the selected feature takes precedence over the possibly conflicting ones.

Despite the similarities between the inheritance scheme in Eiffel and the composition scheme of stateful traits, there are some significant differences:

– *Renaming vs. aliasing* – In Eiffel, when a subclass is created, inherited features can be renamed. Renaming a feature has the same effect as (i) giving a new name to this feature and (ii) changing all the references to this feature. This implies a kind of mapping to be performed when a renamed method is accessed through the static type of the superclass.

For instance, let's assume a class Component defines a method update. A subclass GraphicalComponent renames update into repaint, and redefines this repaint with a new implementation. The following code illustrates this situation:

```
class Component                          class GraphicalComponent
feature                                  inherit
    update is                                Component
        do                                       rename
            print ('1')                              update as repaint
        end                                      redefine
end                                              repaint
                                             end
                                         repaint is
                                             do
                                                 print ('2')
                                             end
                                         end
```

In essence, the method repaint acts as an override of update. It means that if update is sent to an instance of GraphicalComponent, then repaint is called. This is illustrated in the following example:

```
f (c: Component) is
    do
        c.update
    end
f (create{GraphicalComponent})
==> 2
```

This is the way Eiffel preserves polymorphism while supporting renaming.

In stateful traits, aliasing a method or granting access to a variable assigns a new name to it. The method or the variable can therefore still be invoked or accessed through its original name.

- *Merging variables* – In contrast to to stateful traits, variables can be merged in Eiffel only if they provide from a common superclass. In stateful traits, variables provided by two traits can be merged regardless of how these traits are formed.

Jigsaw. Jigsaw [Bra92] has a module system in which a module is a self-referential scope that binds names to values (*i.e.*, constant and functions). A module acts as a class (object generator) and as a coarse-grained structural software unit. Modules can be nested, therefore a module can define a set of classes. A set of operators is provided to compose modules. These operators are instantiation, merge, override, rename, restrict, and freeze.

Although there are some differences between the definition of a Jigsaw module and stateful traits, for instance with the rename operator, the more significant differences are in motivation and setting. Jigsaw is a framework for defining modular languages. Jigsaw supports full renaming, and assigns a semantic interpretation to nesting. In Jigsaw, a renaming is equivalent to a textual replacement of all occurrences of the attribute. The *rename* operator distributes over *override*. It means that Jigsaw has the following property:

(m1 rename a to b) override (m2 rename a to b) = (m1 override m2) rename a to b

Traits are intended to supplement existing languages by promoting reuse in the small, do not declare types, infer their requirements, and do not allow renaming. Stateless traits do not assign any meaning to nesting. Stateful traits are sensitive to nesting only to the extent that instance variables are private to a given scope. The Jigsaw operation set also aims for completeness, whereas in the design of traits we sacrifice completeness for simplicity.

A notable difference between Jigsaw and stateful traits is with the merging of variables. In Jigsaw, a module can have state, however variables cannot be shared between modules. With stateful traits the same variable can be accessed by the traits that use it. A Jigsaw module acts as a black-box. A module encapsulates its bindings and cannot be opened. While we value black-box composition, stateful traits do not take such a restrictive approach, but rather let the client assume responsibility for the composition, while being protected from the impact of changes.

It is worth mentioning typing issues raised when implementing Jigsaw. Bracha [Bra92, Chapter 7] pointed out that the difficulty in implementing inheritance in Jigsaw (which is operator-based) stems from the interaction between structural subtyping and the algebraic properties of the inheritance operators (*e.g.*, *merge* and *override*).

For example, let's consider the following classes A, B, C, D, E and F where C is a subclass of A and B. E is a subclass of D and C. F is a subclass of D, A and B. We have $C = AB$, $E = DC$ and $F = DAB$ where in $C_{new} = C_1 C_2 ... C_n$ the superclasses of C_{new} are denoted C_i. (See Figure 13.) Expanding the definitions of all names (as dictated by structural typing), one finds that by associativity $E = F$. This equivalence dictates that all three classes have the same type, so that they can be used interchangeably. This in turn requires that all three have the same representation.

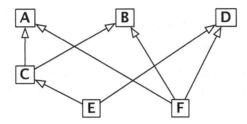

Fig. 13. E and F are structurally equivalent but may have different representations

However, using the techniques of C++ (Section 5.3), these three classes have different representations. This problem is avoided in traits where a trait does not define a type.

Cecil. Cecil [Cha92] is a purely object-oriented language that combines a classless object model, a kind of dynamic inheritance and an optional static type checking. Cecil's static type system distinguishes between subtyping and code inheritance even if the more common case is when the subtyping hierarchy parallels the inheritance hierarchy. Cecil supports multiple inheritance. Inheriting from the same ancestor more than once, whether directly or indirectly, has no effect other than to place the ancestor in relation to other ancestors: Cecil has no repeated inheritance. Inheritance in Cecil requires a child to accept all of the fields and methods defined in the parents. These fields and methods may be overridden in the child, but facilities such as excluding fields or methods from the parents or renaming them as part of the inheritance are not present in Cecil. This is an important difference with respect to stateful traits.

9   Conclusion

Stateless traits offer a simple compositional approach for structuring object-oriented programs. A trait is essentially a group of pure methods that serves as a building block for classes and as a primitive unit of code reuse. However this simple model suffers from several limitations, in particular (i) trait reusability is impacted because the required interface is typically cluttered with uninteresting required accessors, (ii) client classes are forced to implement boilerplate glue code, (iii) the introduction of new state in a trait propagates required accessors to all client classes, and (iv) public accessors break encapsulation of the client class.

We have proposed a way to make traits *stateful* as follows: First, traits can have private variables. Second, classes or traits composed from traits may use the *variable access operator* to (i) access variables of the used traits, (ii) attribute local names to those variables, and (iii) merge variables of multiple used traits, when this is desired. The flattening property can be preserved by alpha-renaming variable names that clash.

Stateful traits offer numerous benefits: There is no unnecessary propagation of required methods, traits can encapsulate their internal representation, and the client can identify the essential required methods more clearly. Duplicated boilerplate glue code is no longer needed. A trait encapsulates its own state, therefore an evolving trait does not break its clients if its public interface remains unmodified.

Stateful traits represent a relatively modest extension to single-inheritance languages that enables the expression of classes as compositions of fine-grained, reusable software components. An open question for further study is whether trait composition can subsume class-based inheritance, leading to a programming language based on composition rather than inheritance as the primary mechanism for structuring code following Jigsaw design.

Acknowledgment

We gratefully acknowledge the financial support of the Swiss National Science Foundation for the project "A Unified Approach to Composition and Extensibility" (SNF Project No. 200020-105091/1), and of the Science Foundation Ireland and Lero — the Irish Software Engineering Research Centre.

We also thank Nathanel Schärli, Gilad Bracha, Bernd Schoeller , Dave Thomas and Orla Greevy for their valuable discussions and comments. Thanks to Ian Joyner for his help with the MacOSX Eiffel implementation.

References

[BC90]   Gilad Bracha and William Cook. Mixin-based inheritance. In *Proceedings OOP-SLA/ECOOP '90, ACM SIGPLAN Notices*, volume 25, pages 303–311, October 1990.

[BGG+02] Lars Bak, Gilad Bracha Steffen Grarup, Robert Griesemer, David Griswold, and Urs Hölzle. Mixins in Strongtalk. In *ECOOP '02 Workshop on Inheritance*, June 2002.

[Bra92]   Gilad Bracha. *The Programming Language Jigsaw: Mixins, Modularity and Multiple Inheritance*. PhD thesis, Dept. of Computer Science, University of Utah, March 1992.

[BSD03]   Andrew P. Black, Nathanael Schärli, and Stéphane Ducasse. Applying traits to the Smalltalk collection hierarchy. In *Proceedings OOPSLA'03 (International Conference on Object-Oriented Programming Systems, Languages and Applications)*, volume 38, pages 47–64, October 2003.

[CDG+92] Luca Cardelli, Jim Donahue, Lucille Glassman, Mick Jordan, Bill Kalsow, and Greg Nelson. Modula-3 language definition. *ACM SIGPLAN Notices*, 27(8):15–42, August 1992.

[Cha92]   Craig Chambers. Object-oriented multi-methods in cecil. In O. Lehrmann Madsen, editor, *Proceedings ECOOP '92*, volume 615 of *LNCS*, pages 33–56, Utrecht, the Netherlands, June 1992. Springer-Verlag.

[DNS+06] Stéphane Ducasse, Oscar Nierstrasz, Nathanael Schärli, Roel Wuyts, and Andrew Black. Traits: A mechanism for fine-grained reuse. *ACM Transactions on Programming Languages and Systems*, 28(2):331–388, March 2006.

[for]   The fortress language specification. http://research.sun.com/projects/plrg/fortress0866.pdf.

[FR03]   Kathleen Fisher and John Reppy. Statically typed traits. Technical Report TR-2003-13, University of Chicago, Department of Computer Science, December 2003.

[IKM⁺97]   Dan Ingalls, Ted Kaehler, John Maloney, Scott Wallace, and Alan Kay. Back to the future: The story of Squeak, A practical Smalltalk written in itself. In *Proceedings OOPSLA '97, ACM SIGPLAN Notices*, pages 318–326. ACM Press, November 1997.

[Jik]   The jikes research virtual machine. http://jikesrvm.sourceforge.net/.

[Kro85]   S. Krogdahl. Multiple inheritance in simula-like languages. In *BIT 25*, pages 318–326, 1985.

[Mey92]   Bertrand Meyer. *Eiffel: The Language*. Prentice-Hall, 1992.

[Moh02]   Markus Mohnen. Interfaces with default implementations in Java. In *Conference on the Principles and Practice of Programming in Java*, pages 35–40. ACM Press, Dublin, Ireland, jun 2002.

[NDS06]   Oscar Nierstrasz, Stéphane Ducasse, and Nathanael Schärli. Flattening Traits. *Journal of Object Technology*, 5(4):129–148, May 2006.

[Pyt]   Python. http://www.python.org.

[sca]   Scala home page. http://lamp.epfl.ch/scala/.

[SD05]   Charles Smith and Sophia Drossopoulou. Chai: Typed traits in Java. In *Proceedings ECOOP 2005*, 2005.

[SDNB03]   Nathanael Schärli, Stéphane Ducasse, Oscar Nierstrasz, and Andrew Black. Traits: Composable units of behavior. In *Proceedings ECOOP 2003 (European Conference on Object-Oriented Programming)*, volume 2743 of *LNCS*, pages 248–274. Springer Verlag, July 2003.

[SE90]   Bjarne Stroustrup and Magaret A. Ellis. *The Annotated C++ Reference Manual*. Addison Wesley, 1990.

[SG99]   Peter F. Sweeney and Joseph (Yossi) Gil. Space and time-efficient memory layout for multiple inheritance. In *Proceedings OOPSLA '99*, pages 256–275. ACM Press, 1999.

[Sla]   Slate. http://slate.tunes.org.

[Sny86]   Alan Snyder. Encapsulation and inheritance in object-oriented programming languages. In *Proceedings OOPSLA '86, ACM SIGPLAN Notices*, volume 21, pages 38–45, November 1986.

[UCCH91]   David Ungar, Craig Chambers, Bay-Wei Chang, and Urs Hölzle. Organizing programs without classes. *LISP and SYMBOLIC COMPUTATION: An international journal*, 4(3), 1991.

[US87]   David Ungar and Randall B. Smith. Self: The power of simplicity. In *Proceedings OOPSLA '87, ACM SIGPLAN Notices*, volume 22, pages 227–242, December 1987.

SCL:
A Simple, Uniform and Operational Language for Component-Oriented Programming in Smalltalk

Luc Fabresse, Christophe Dony, and Marianne Huchard

Lirmm, UMR 5506 CNRS et Université Montpellier II
161, rue Ada
34392 Montpellier Cedex 5
{fabresse,dony,huchard}@lirmm.fr
http://www.lirmm.fr

Abstract. Unanticipated connection of independently developed components is one of the key issues in component-oriented programming. While a variety of component-oriented languages have been proposed, none of them has achieved a breakthrough yet.

In this paper, we present SCL a simple language dedicated to component-oriented programming. SCL integrates well-known features such as component class, component, interface, port or service. All these well-known features are presented, discussed and compared to existing approaches because they vary quite widely from one language to another. But, these features are not enough to build a component language. Indeed, most approaches use language primitives and shared interfaces to connect components. But shared interfaces are in contradiction with the philosophy of independently developed components. To this issue, SCL provides new features such as a *uniform component composition model* based on *connectors*. Connectors represent interactions between independently developed components. SCL also integrates *component properties* which enable connections based on component state changes with no requirements of specific code in components.

Keywords: component-oriented programming, unanticipated composition, connector, component property.

1 Introduction

Component-based software engineering is widely investigated by research and industry. This interest is driven by the promise of improving current software development practices in significant ways such as reusability and extensibility [23,45]. Although many models, languages and tools have been proposed, it is still difficult to apply component-oriented programming (COP) in practice. Most of these languages are not executable and dedicated to software specification such

W. De Meuter (Ed.): ISC 2006, LNCS 4406, pp. 91–110, 2007.
© Springer-Verlag Berlin Heidelberg 2007

as UML 2.0 [21] or architecture description such as WRIGHT [5,4]. COP is currently carried out using object-oriented languages. These languages do not offer specific abstractions to ease COP and have to be used in a disciplined way to guarantee a COP style.

Component-based software engineering needs component-oriented languages (COL) as well as transformation of models [37,12] into executables or writing programs by hand [16]. Among the approaches on components, component-oriented languages have been proposed in order to support COP such as ComponentJ [42], ArchJava [2], Julia/Fractal [8], Lagoona [16], Piccola [1], Picolo [30], Boxscript [29], Keris [48] or Koala [46]. The contributions of these languages are new or adapted abstractions and mechanisms that vary quite widely from one proposal to another such as connection, composition, port, interface, connector, service, module, message, etc. This is quite normal with such an emerging domain, but there is a need for a closer analysis: which mechanisms are essential (basic) and cannot be removed, which ones are (eventually) redundant? Which are the key ones to achieve component composition? To a larger extent, all these questions raise the issue of knowing which constructs and mechanisms are the main identified features of component orientation (by analogy with object orientation).

In this paper, we propose SCL that stands for Simple Component Language which is the result of our study and research of component-oriented programming. SCL is built on a minimal set of concepts applied uniformly in order to ease the understanding of key concepts of component-oriented programming. Picolo [30] and BoxScript [29] are two languages that also target this goal of minimality for simplicity. However, SCL integrates a more powerful and extensible component composition mechanism which is one of the key mechanisms of COP. In SCL, component composition relies on first-class entities representing connections, named *connectors* [43,33]. Connectors offer better decoupling between the business code inside components and the connection code inside connectors, and thus increase the reuse of components. Some COL already propose connectors such as ArchJava [2] or Sofa [6], but SCL connectors offer more expressiveness by integrating ideas that come from aspect-oriented programming [26]. SCL also proposes the concept of *property* to externalize component state without breaking component encapsulation. Properties are the support of a new kind of component communication that is based on changes of property state. Properties ease the use of the publish-subscribe communication pattern without requiring any special code in the publisher or the subscriber. We choose Squeak, a Smalltalk implementation, to implement SCL because it is a dynamic language that offers a suitable meta-object protocol that can be easily extended. Although it is also possible to implement SCL in another language, we choose to experiment COP in a dynamic context and we want to provide an easily extensible language.

The paper is organized as follows. Section 2 presents basic ideas of component-oriented programming. Section 3 details main characteristics of the SCL language: component classes, components, ports, interfaces, connectors and properties.

Section 4 presents the current implementation of SCL in Squeak. Section 5 discusses related work. Finally, Section 6 concludes and presents future work.

2   Component-Oriented Programming: What, Why and How ?

Component-oriented programming (COP) does for decoupling software entities what object-oriented programming has done for object encapsulation and inheritance, or aspect-oriented programming has done for crosscutting concerns. It provides language mechanisms that explicitly capture software architecture structures. COP is based on the idea stating that software can be built by plugging pieces of software called *components*. The term "component" means many different things to many different people depending upon the perspective taken on the development. For example, design patterns [17], functions or procedures [31], modules [16], application frameworks [45], object-oriented classes [22], and whole applications [34] are considered as components. Similarly, there are many different definitions for the term component given in the literature [7,20,45]. In this paper, we use the following definition : *"A software component is a unit of composition with contractually specified interfaces and explicit context dependencies only. A software component can be deployed independently and is subject to composition by third parties"* [45].

Component-based software development focuses on better reuse and easier evolution. A component must be independent of one particular context in order to be reusable. Furthermore, reusing a component is better than creating it from scratch because it has already been developed and tested. The evolution and maintenance of a component software architecture may be easier than a class hierarchy. This is because of the *independent extensibility* [45] property of component-based software. Indeed, component-based applications are built out of interconnected components and each component can evolve independently.

3   The Scl Language

In this section we describe SCL (Simple Component Language). We present and motivate its main features and discuss the problems that arise when designing a COL.

3.1   Component Classes and Component Instances

In object-oriented languages, the terms "class" and "instance" allow programmers to refer without ambiguity respectively to object descriptions in code and to objects themselves as runtime entities. Although component-based languages are generally built on a class/instance conceptual model, few of them specify the terms to denote respectively component classes and component objects. Moreover, there is no widely accepted terms in component-oriented approaches because there is not a unique definition of the component term. For example, the two keywords **component class** in ArchJava and **component** in ComponentJ denote a component class which can be instantiated. Component classes are at the same time component descriptors, component instantiators and component method holders such as in ArchJava. Few COLs have been proposed with a prototype-based model i.e without descriptors such as in [47] where a prototype-based language has been proposed on the top of Java in order to provide primitives to dynamically build, extend and compose software components from Java objects. We think that the arguments for the use (or not) of classes is similar in the component and object worlds and that both approaches are worth to be considered. In SCL, we have chosen a class/instance approach. A *component* is a runtime entity and it is an instance of a *component class*. Component classes are written by the *component programmer* in order to create off-the-shelf reusable pieces of software while the *software architect* creates an application by choosing some component classes and then connecting instances i.e components. Figure 1 shows the code to create a component class and the code to create a component using the **new** message.

```
SCLCOMPONENTCLASSBUILDER  create: #MyComponent.
. . .
c := MYCOMPONENT new.
. . .
```

Fig. 1. A component descriptor and a component instance

3.2   Component Provisions and Requirements

Component interfaces and services. As stated by Szyperski [45], a component can only be accessed through well-defined *interfaces*. Component interfaces enforce explicit context-dependencies and a high-level of encapsulation. A component interface describes only a *service* or a group of services provided by a component to other components. A component provides a lot of services through different interfaces but its clients can only use those ones defined in the interface which they are connected to. Component interfaces also specify the services that are required by a component to be able to provide its own services. Basically, a service is a subprogram defined in a component, such as a method in the object-oriented model. The term service is used to refer to a high-level functionality. For example, a *Network* service is at least composed of four methods: **open:** to initialize a network connection, **close** to finish the connection, **send:** and **receive** to respectively send and receive data through an open connection. Component-based languages propose different concepts to describe component interfaces such as ports, interfaces, protocols, etc. In SCL, we choose to represent component interfaces by *ports* described by *interfaces*. We argue that these two concepts are enough to describe component interfaces.

Ports. Ports represent interaction points of a component such as in Arch-Java [2] or ComponentJ [42]. The port construct has not the same definition and characteristics in all COLs. For example in Picolo, ComponentJ or Fractal (ports are called external interfaces in Fractal), ports are *unidirectional* because they provide or require a set of services. In ArchJava or UML 2.0 [11], ports are *bi-directional* and the component invokes external services and receives service invocations through the same port. Required services through a port have to be provided by the same component. For example, a component that requires a *Network* service through one of its ports, expects services **open:** , **send:**, **receive** and **close**, will be executed by the same component. However, provided services are accessible to one or many other components. Providing and requiring services through one port may result in limiting the use of the provided services to only one component at a time. SCL integrates two kinds of unidirectional ports: those ones for accessing required services and those ones for giving access to provided services. A port has a name. A component can not have two ports with the same name. A port name is used in the code to specify through which port a service is invoked. A service is always invoked through a port by message sending (the same term as in object world is used). Syntactically, the port is the receiver but in fact, the real receiver of a message is always a component that will be known at connection time. Note that it is worth to invoke a service that the component itself defines. All components have a special internal provided port named **self** that can not be accessed outside of the component. In this context, the invocation **self foo** is equivalent to a service invocation that requires no connection to be achieved and that executes the **foo** service of current component. To sum up, an SCL component offers or requires *services*, receives or sends *service invocation*, and can be *connected* through its ports as we will see later in Section 3.3.

Interfaces. An interface describes the valid interactions through a port in order to document the component or to enable the automatic validation (static or dynamic) of the component uses and the connections. In COLs, these descriptions vary from simple ones such as informal texts in natural languages to complex ones such as formal descriptions. These descriptions are classified in two categories: syntactic and semantic.

Syntactical descriptions are generally represented using *interfaces* (such as in Java). An interface defines a named type describing a set of method signatures. Validation of the use of a port relies on typing rules. For example, a port that requires an interface I_1 can be connected with a port that provides an interface I_2 where the type defined by I_1 is a supertype of the one defined by I_2. Using interfaces implies that independently developed software components have to refer to a common standard defined by interfaces in order to inter-operate. Other solutions exist, such as structural type systems [10], that offer better decoupling between component classes. But structural type systems are less expressive than named type systems (such as with interfaces) as said in [9], *"[...] types stand for semantical specification. While the conformance of an implementation to a behavioral specification cannot be easily checked by current compilers, type conformance is checkable. By simply comparing names, compilers can check that several parties refer to the same standard specification."*. For example, writing that "a component requires a stack" is more expressive than writing that "a component requires two services pop and push:" but in the first case there is a need for a global stack definition.

Semantical descriptions are harder to define and are often based on formal theory, such as CSP in WRIGHT [5] or protocols in Sofa [40]. For example, protocols allow component programmers to define the valid sequences of service invocations through regular expressions. In our last example of the Network service, it is important to describe that firstly the open: service has to be invoked, then the send: and receive services can be used, and finally the close service must be invoked to finish the interaction.

Ports and Interfaces in Scl. We choose to decouple component classes and avoid global definitions such as named interfaces. This is the reason why interfaces are service signature sets in SCL and not named interfaces. But, it is possible to extend SCL to support more sophisticated interfaces as protocols. Figure 2 shows an example of component class with ports and Figure 3 shows the SCL code needed to declare it. PASSWORDMANAGER is a component class created by the bootstrap method SCLCOMPONENTBUILDER>>create: that creates an empty component class. In its internal service named init, the PASSWORDMANAGER is composed of three ports: Randomizing is a required port since it is used to invoke external services of the component; Generating and Checking are required ports because they offer some services of the component and receive service invocations from third parties. Since we do not focus on static or dynamic validation of connections, it is not mandatory to specify interfaces of required ports. The same situation happens in dynamically-typed languages when method parameters are not described by a static type. However, interfaces of provided ports are needed because they specify which services of the components are provided through the port.

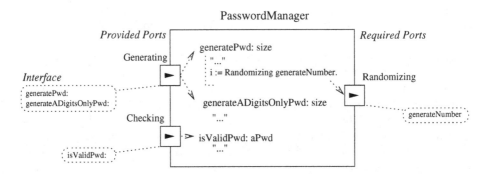

Fig. 2. A SCL component. Ports are represented by squares on the component boundary and triangles designate the direction of service invocations. Ports are described by interfaces which are service signature sets.

```
SCLCOMPONENTCLASSBUILDER create: #PasswordManager.

PASSWORDMANAGER>>init
   self addPort: (SclPort newNamed: #Randomizing requires:
      (SclInterface new with: {#generateNumber})).
   self addPort: (SclPort newNamed: #Generating provides:
      (SclInterface new with: {
         #generatePwd:.
         #generateADigitsOnlyPwd:
      })).
   self addPort: (SclPort newNamed: #Checking provides:
      (SclInterface new with: {#isValidPassword:})).

PASSWORDMANAGER>>generatePwd: size
   "..."
   i := Randomizing generateNumber.
   "..."
```

Fig. 3. A component class declaration

3.3   Component Composition

There are two main mechanisms for unanticipated composition of components: *connection* and *composition*[1]. **Unanticipated** is the key-adjective attached to composition or connection that makes component-based software worthwhile. To be composable, a component definition should only state what it provides and what it needs and should make no assumption about which other concrete components it will be composed with later on.

Connection. As said in [36], *"a component is a static abstraction with plugs"*. In SCL, plugs of components are their ports. The **connection** is the mechanism that connects component ports. The connection mechanism is provided through various forms in actual COLs, e.g. the `connect` primitive and connectors in ArchJava [3], the `plug` primitive in ComponentJ [42], connectors in Picolo [30] or bindings in Fractal [8]. Connections are the support for the communication between components and they enforce the decoupling between components which can not communicate if they have not been connected.

Connection mismatches are identified consequences of unanticipated connections [41]. These mismatches occur when we want to connect components that semantically fit well but their connection is not possible because they are not plug-compatible. Mismatches can be solved in whole generality by defining dedicated components as specified by the Adapter design pattern [17]. There is a need for glue code in connections to adapt components. A connection mechanism must be flexible to make the definition of adapters useless.

Connecting components could be achieved using language primitives such as plug in ComponentJ [42]. Other component models propose connections as first-class entities named *connectors* such as Sofa [6] or ArchJava [3] and most of Architecture Description Languages [32], such as WRIGHT [5,4]. Connectors are

---

[1] The term *composition* is used here for a mechanism that creates a new component out of existing ones.

architectural building blocks used to model interactions among components and rules that govern those interactions [43]. Unlike components, connectors may not correspond to compilation units or deployment units. In SCL, SCLCONNECTOR is the most general form of connectors which is composed of two sets of ports named *sources* and *targets* and *glue code* that only uses these ports to establish the connection. SCLCALLCONNECTOR is the general connector dedicated to service invocation connections as shown in Figure 4.

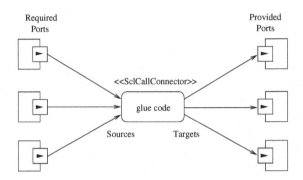

Fig. 4. The general form a SCL connector

In a SCLCALLCONNECTOR, sources are required ports and targets are provided ports. It is possible to define specialized connectors that provide a general purpose glue code or restrict sources and targets. Among the various existing connector types, there is one, SCLBINARYCONNECTOR that restricts itself to one source and one target. Figure 5 shows an example of binary connection between a PASSWORDMANAGER component and a RANDOMNUMBERGENERATOR component. This connection satisfies the required service of the PASSWORDMANAGER through its `Randomizing` port, using the service `generateNumber` provided by the RANDOMNUMBERGENERATOR through its `Generating` port. Figure 6 shows the code to establish this connection.

The glue code of a SCLCALLCONNECTOR is a Smalltalk block whose parameters are the set of sources, the set of targets and the current service invocation (which includes the source port, the selector and parameters) that has to be performed. In the glue code of this example, the result of the `rand` service is adapted since the `generatedpassword` is expected to return a number in the interval $[0, 26]$ while the `rand` service returns a number in the interval $[0, 1]$. Despite of the fact that this is a simple example, it is important to note that connecting independently developed software components must deal with these kinds of problems. The glue code in connectors is a good place to tackle these adaptation problems. If no glue code is specified in a SCLBINARYCONNECTOR, the default behavior is to forward all services that come from the source port to the target port and to return the result. This is the same as the Fractal *bind* primitive or the ComponentJ `plug` primitive.

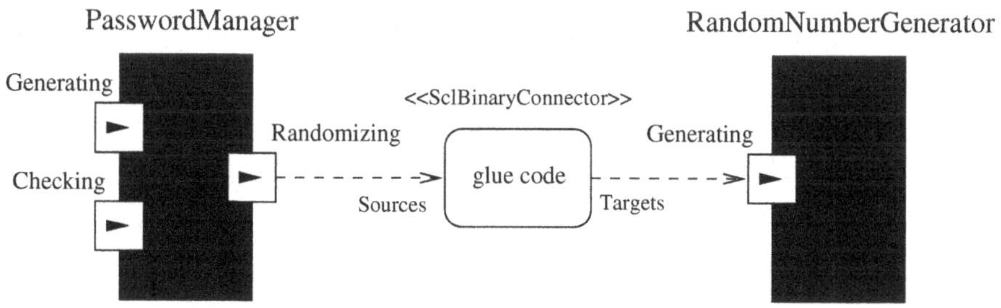

Fig. 5. A Scl connection of two components

Like the SclBinaryConnector, it is possible to build reusable connectors, such as BroadcasterConnector, that broadcasts each service invocation to all targets, or FirstResultConnector that returns the first non-nil result by sending invocation successively to each target.

```
spm := PasswordManager new.
srng := RandomNumberGenerator new.
SclBinaryConnector new
   source: (spm port: #Randomizing)
   target: (srng port: #Generating)
   glue: [ :source :target :message |
       ^(target rand * 26) asInteger
       ];
   connect.
```

Fig. 6. Connecting two components

Composition. Composition is the mechanism that builds a composite component out of components and connections. Encapsulated components are generally called sub-components of the composite. Composite components are useful to abstract over complex systems and provide a new reusable software entity that hide implementation details. This mechanism is provided through various forms in existing languages, e.g the **compose** primitive in ComponentJ [42], composite components in Fractal or aggregation and containment in (D)COM [34].

Figure 7 and Figure 8 show the architecture and the code of a simple composite in Scl. A composite component c instance of the component class C encapsulates two components a and b and one connection. Each instance of C *forwards* the provided port **pb** of its subcomponent b for external uses. This example is quite simple and more complex ones require the use of SclForwardConnector s. These kinds of connectors are used to forward externalize services of sub-components in a composite component. The sources and targets are all required or provided ports and the glue code can be used to solve problems such as name conflicts, etc. Figure 9 and Figure 10 shows this situation with a composite component that provides two services on a same port but provided by two different sub-components.

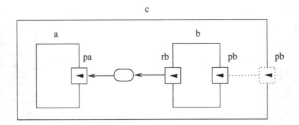

Fig. 7. A composite component that forwards a port

3.4   Separation of Concerns in Component Applications

Separation of concerns [38] principle states that a software system should be modularized in such a way that different concerns can be specified as independent as possible in order to maximize understandability and maintenability. Some concerns are difficult to encapsulate in standard software units (components or objects), such as management of transactions, logs, security, etc. To tackle the problem of the scattered code of these concerns, aspect-oriented programming [26] introduces *aspects*. An aspect is the modularization of a crosscutting concern. Two approaches are distinguished in AOP. Asymmetric approaches consider aspects as different entities from those ones that compose the base system (objects or components), such as AspectJ [25], or JAsCo [44]. Symmetric approaches try to use the same entities to model the base system and aspects. This second approach is better for reusability because if aspects are modeled as components, they can be used as regular components as well as aspects. A lot of approaches try to merge in a symmetric way aspect-oriented and component-oriented approaches to benefit from the modular properties of both approaches, such as Fractal-AOP [14] or FAC [39].

In SCL, we adopt a symmetric approach with limited aspect-oriented features which are provided through special connectors and ports characteristics. The *join points* – well defined points in the execution of a program where aspects can be woven – are generally method calls, method call receptions, method executions or attribute accesses. The supported joint points in SCL are: before/after/around a service invocation or connection/disconnection on a port. Figure 11 shows an example that uses an SCLFLOWCONNECTOR and a regular LOGGER component to add the logging support to a component c through its port pc.

In a SCLFLOWCONNECTOR, all source ports are coupled with a keyword (beforeServiceInvocation, beforeConnection, ...) that specifies when the glue code has to be executed. At execution time, when a service invocation arrives on a port, glue code of attached connectors are executed in the same order as in AOP (around, before, after). Conflicts are possible, for example if multiple glue codes have to be executed before a service invocation on the same port, the glue code of the last connected connector will be executed first. This rule lets the architect deal with potential weaving problems.

```
SCLCOMPONENTCLASSBUILDER createComposite: #C.

C>>init
    self addSubComponent: A new named: a.
    self addSubComponent: B new named: b.
    self forwardPort: (b port: #pb).

    SCLBINARYCONNECTOR new
        source: (b port: #rb)
        target: (a port: #pa) ;
        connect.
```

Fig. 8. Declaration of a composite component class

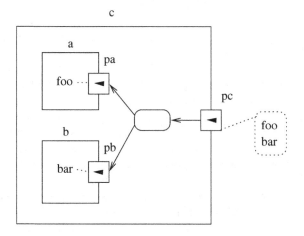

Fig. 9. Port forwarding using a connector

```
SCLCOMPONENTCLASSBUILDER createComposite: #C.

C>>init
    self addSubComponent: #A named: a.
    self addSubComponent: #B named: b.
    self addPort: (SclPort new: #pc
            provides: (SclInterface new with: {#foo. #bar})).

    SCLFORWARDCONNECTOR new
        sources:{self port: #pc}
        targets:(b port: #pb).
           (a port: #pa)}
        glue: [ :sources :targets :message |
          (message selector == #foo) ifTrue:[
            ^targets first perform: message
          ] ifFalse: [
            (message selector == #bar) ifTrue:[
               ^targets second perform: message
            ].
          ].
        ];
        connect.
```

Fig. 10. Using a connector to forward services in a composite component

```
l := Logger new.

SclFlowBinaryConnector new
   source:((c port: #pc) beforeServiceInvocation)
   target:(l port: #Logging)
   glue: [ :source :target :message |
      target log: 'The ', message selector, ' message will be sent to a'
   ];
   connect.
```

Fig. 11. Modify the control flow using a connector

3.5   Component Properties and Publish/Subscribe Connections

Triggering operations as a consequence of state changes in a component is related to Observer design pattern [17] or *procedural attachments* [35]. In frame languages, it is possible to attach procedures to an attribute access which is then executed each time this attribute is accessed. These kinds of interactions are particularly used between "views" (in the MVC sense [27]) and "models". More generally, the publish/subscribe [13] communication protocol is a very useful communication pattern to decouple software entities as said in [18]: *"The main invariant in this style is announcers of events do not know which components will be affected by those events"*. In component-based languages, this must be done in an unanticipated way and with strict separation between the component code and the connection code to enable components reuse. However, existing proposals fail to solve these two main constraints. Connecting components based on event notifications always require that component programmers add special code in components. We identify the two following problems:

Publishers have to publish events. The component programmer has to add special code such as event signaling in components. For example, in the *Java Bean* model, the programmer has to manage explicitly the subscribers list (add and remove subscriber methods). In the CCM (Corba Component Model), the component programmer has to manage the event sending by adding a special port to his component that is called an *event source*, and sends events in the component code through this port. In ArchJava, the component programmer declares broadcast methods (required methods that return void) and invokes them in the component code to signal events. This method is then connected by the architect to multiple provided methods of subscriber components that receive the events. In all cases, the architect can not reuse a component if its programmer has not added special code in the component to signal the event that he needs.

Emitters have to receive events. In the CCM, the component programmer has to provide its components with *event sinks* that are special ports to receive events. An event sink can be connected by the architect with one or more event sources if they share a compatible event type. This mechanism is more limiting than the ArchJava or the Javabeans one where the subscriber components have only regular methods that are invoked using connections.

In order to increase the component reuse, we have to decouple the connection code from the business code written by the component programmer. The programmer has to focus on the business code and the design of the component i.e what it requires and what it provides. In SCL, there are three ways to enable publish/subscribe connections:

1. The component programmer integrates the event signaling in the component code. Event signaling in SCL can be done, similarly as in ArchJava, by invoking a required service in the publisher component and using regular SCLCALLCONNECTOR to link publishers and subscribers.
2. The component programmer does not integrate the event signaling in the component code and SCLFLOWCONNECTORS can be used by the architect to detect the events that he needs. For example, if the architect wants to detect when a stack becomes empty (an EmptyStackEvent), he can use an AFTERCONNECTOR on the port that provides the **pop** service and test in the glue code if the stack still contains elements to detect such situation.
3. The component programmer has declared *properties*. This property concept enhances the idea of property of the Javabeans component model [22] with strict separation between component code and connection code. A property is an external state of a component. For example, a COUNTER component has a property named **count**. This means that it is possible to get and set a value to the **count** property of the COUNTER. Figure 12 shows the SCL code for this declaration.

```
SCLCOMPONENTCLASSBUILDER  create:  #Counter.

COUNTER>>init
  self  addAttribute:  #value.
  self  addPort:  (SclPort new:  #Counting
           provides:  (SclInterface  new  with:  {#dec.  #inc})).
  self  addProperty:  #Count read:  [^value]  write:  [ :nv |  value := nv ].

C>>inc
  self  count:  (self  count + 1)

C>>dec
  self  count:  (self  count − 1)
```

Fig. 12. A Counter component class with a property

When a programmer declares a property, the component is automatically composed of two ports: an *access port* and a *notifying port*. The property access port is a provided port that provides, at least, getter and setter services using the two blocks given during the property declaration. The notifying port is a required port, which is used to invoke services during property accesses. These services are defined in the SCL component model. For example, the service **nac:value:oldValue:** (nac is an acronym for Notify After Change) is invoked

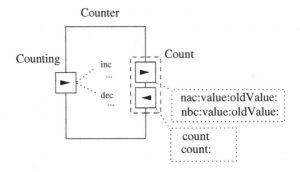

Fig. 13. A counter component with a value property

```
gui := LABEL new.
counter := COUNTER new.

SCLBINARYNACCONNECTOR new
   source: ( counter notifyPortOf: #Count)
   target: ( gui port: #Displaying )
   glue: [ :source :gui :message |
      gui displayText: (message arguments second).
   ]; connect.
```

Fig. 14. A state changes connection based on a component property

after a property is modified with the new and the old value of the property as parameters. Another service, the `nbc:value:newValue:` (nbc is an acronym for Notify Before Change) service, is invoked before the property is modified with the current value and the next value of the property as parameters. In fact, all defined services have two main characteristics: when they are invoked (before or after the property modification) and what a connected component is able to do (nothing, prevent the modification or change the property value). Special or regular connectors can be used to connect properties since they are just two regular ports. An example of connection using properties is depicted on Figure 13 and the corresponding SCL code is shown on Figure 14.

In this example, a SCLBINARYNACCONNECTOR is used. This connector filters incoming service invocations on the source port and only focuses on the `nac:value:oldValue` service. After each modification of the value property of the counter, the glue code of the connection is executed and the GUI component is refreshed with the new value (the second parameter of the `nac:value:oldValue` service). Actually, SCL provides different kinds of connectors like SCLBINARYNACCONNECTOR, SCLBINARYNBCCONNECTOR, PROPERTY-BINDERCONNECTOR ensuring that the value of the target property is always synchronized with the value of the source property. To sum up, component properties are a useful means for component programmers to directly express the external state of components instead of using syntactical conventions and for architects that can use them to connect components.

4 Implementation

The actual prototype of SCL [28] is implemented in Squeak/Smalltalk [24]. Squeak is an open and highly portable implementation based on the original Smalltalk-80 system [19]. Figure 15 shows a part of the class diagram of the core model.

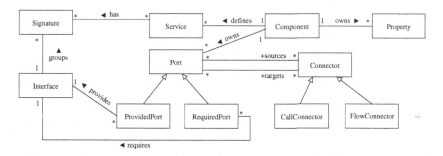

Fig. 15. UML class diagram of the current implementation of SCL

This figure shows only main connector families. In [33], a taxonomy of software connectors has been established and eight kinds of connectors have been identified. Similarly to the work done for ArchJava in [3], we have implemented connectors of each kind. This shows that the connector model of SCL is suitable to perform a large variety of connectors.

The current SCL syntax is the same as the Smalltalk one although some changes in semantics have been done. For example, the syntactical receiver of a service invocation is a port but the real Smalltalk receiver is not this port but the component which this port belongs to. Because we do not implement SCL with an evaluator or a compiler but directly with Smalltalk constructs, it is easier to change and evolve the implementation. It is also difficult to implement special things that are too far from the Smalltalk mechanisms.

5 Related Work

Understanding or teaching COP. Picolo [30] and BoxScript [29] are two frameworks for introducing (teaching) components. Picolo is written in Python and Boxscript in Java. They are small and contrary to SCL, they integrate a simple binary connection mechanism.

Architecture description languages (ADLs). These languages are an important part of the current researches in component-oriented languages. In [32], a classification of the most known ADLs has been established. For example, WRIGHT [5] is one of these languages that integrates connector support. But WRIGHT, as many of these languages, is dedicated to simulation and formal verification. Since ADLs are not executable languages, it is not possible to build an application using it.

ArchJava [2,3] is a Java extension introducing software architecture concepts to express architectural structure of applications within an implementation in order to ensure that the implementation conforms to architectural constraints. ArchJava classes support bidirectional ports in which methods are provided, required or broadcasted. The primitive connection mechanism (connect keyword) is a coarse-grained one because it is based on bidirectional ports. ArchJava does not support properties and component programmers have to write code in components to enable connections based on component state notifications.

Fractal [8] is a recursive and reflective component model. A component has external interfaces (ports) which provides (server interface) or required (client interface) a defined set of services. Components are connected through bindings between external interfaces. A primitive binding is a fixed interface connection mechanism that binds one client interface with one server interface. Binding components also called connectors represent composite bindings to create complex connections. In SCL, components and connectors are different concepts because these two concepts fulfill different purposes, components are the business reusable software units while connectors have to fix connection semantics and deal with connection problems. Julia is the implementation reference of the Fractal model in Java, and Fractalk [15] is an implementation of Fractal in Squeak.

ComponentJ [42] is another Java extension for component-oriented programming. Components provide or require one interface per port. The component programmer defines methods inside method blocks that can be plugged into ports. Plug operations bind one component method block or port to a port according to their interfaces. Component composition is done through dynamic composition (`compose` keyword) and returns a new component. ComponentJ is a strongly typed language ensuring plug operations and composition. There is no connector support in ComponentJ and it is only possible to connect components inside a composite. A component can only be instantiated if it is closed (without unbounded required services) even if all required services are not necessary for the current application.

Javabeans [22] has been one of the first component models allowing programmers to connect independently developed software entities. Javabeans programmers have to write special connection code (essentially Observable code from the Observer pattern) and to respect syntactical rules to ensure that their Javabeans can be automatically connected with other Javabeans using automatic Adaptor [17] generation. Our properties, inspired from the Javabeans model, do not enforce component programmers to write specific connection code.

Component-oriented languages. These languages enable to code an application using a component approach. These languages do not integrate the ADLs features and provide object-oriented extensions to program with components. For example, Lagoona [16] is based on the idea that components are modules that contain class and message definitions. Note that most of proposed component-oriented languages are Java extensions (Lagoona, Keris, ComponentJ, ArchJava, Javabeans, Julia/Fractal, ...). There are few proposals using a dynamic language and none in Smalltalk, except Fractalk that is an implementation of Fractal in Squeak.

Mixing component and aspect oriented programming. As said in section 3.4, we only consider symmetrical approaches such as FAC [39] or Fractal-AOP [14] where aspects are regular components. This is to increase the reuse of components that can be used as regular components as well as aspects components. The specificity of SCL is that nothing is written in a component (no special interface has to be implemented). The architect decides to use a component as a base component or as an aspect component and uses the special connector SCLFLOWCONNECTOR. This SCL feature is clearly not a complete support of AOP, but an attempt to bring some flexibility of AOP in SCL respecting that components are independently developed and composed.

6   Conclusion

Component-based software development is founded on the unanticipated composition of independently developed software components. Such a mechanism must be offered to programmers and many languages integrate some concepts and mechanisms to achieve this. In this paper, we present SCL a concrete component-oriented language. We believe that SCL represents a simple and uniform synthesis of current proposal on component-oriented programming. SCL also brings new features like a general purpose connector model. Connectors are useful to provide an extensible connection mechanism that solves component connection problems. They offer a unified entity that enable standard required/provided connections and also event-based component connections due to special connectors and component properties. A component programmer only declares properties that represent external state of components. A software architect can express connections on the basis of properties notifications with the same connection mechanism based on connectors.

Ongoing researches on SCL are focused on three areas. First, extending the component model of SCL in order to better support dynamically features. For example, dynamically adding or removing ports to a component could be a great solution to deal with components that have a potentially unbounded number of connections such as a Web Server component. Second, we plan to provide a stable release of the current implementation of SCL and integrate tools dedicated to component-oriented programming. And finally, developing large scale applications using SCL will certainly show us interesting results about the SCL expressiveness compared to existing component-oriented languages which are mainly statically typed ones.

References

1. Franz Achermann and Oscar Nierstrasz. Applications = Components + Scripts –
   A Tour of Piccola. In Mehmet Akşit, editor, *Software Architectures and Component Technology*, pages 261–292. Kluwer, 2001.

2. Jonathan Aldrich, Craig Chambers, and David Notkin. ArchJava: Connecting Software Architecture to Implementation. In *ICSE*, pages 187–197. ACM, 2002.
3. Jonathan Aldrich, Vibha Sazawal, Craig Chambers, and David Notkin. Language support for connector abstractions. In Luca Cardelli, editor, *ECOOP*, volume 2743 of *Lecture Notes in Computer Science*, pages 74–102. Springer, 2003.
4. Robert Allen. *A Formal Approach to Software Architecture*. PhD thesis, Carnegie Mellon, School of Computer Science, January 1997. Issued as CMU Technical Report CMU-CS-97-144.
5. Robert Allen and David Garlan. The Wright Architectural Specification Language. Technical report, School of Computer Science, Carnegie Mellon University, Pittsburgh, 1996.
6. Dusan Balek and Frantisek Plasil. Software connectors and their role in component deployment. In *Proceedings of DAIS'01*, Krakow, Poland, September 2001. Kluwer Academic Publishers.
7. Manfred Broy, Anton Deimel, Juergen Henn, Kai Koskimies, Frantisek Plasil, Gustav Pomberger, Wolfgang Pree, Michael Stal, and Clemens A. Szyperski. What characterizes a (software) component? *Software - Concepts and Tools*, 19(1):49–56, 1998.
8. Eric Bruneton, Thierry Coupaye, Matthieu Leclercq, Vivien Quéma, and Jean-Bernard Stefani. An Open Component Model and Its Support in Java. In Ivica Crnkovic, Judith A. Stafford, Heinz W. Schmidt, and Kurt C. Wallnau, editors, *CBSE*, volume 3054 of *Lecture Notes in Computer Science*, pages 7–22. Springer, 2004.
9. Martin Büchi and Wolfgang Weck. Compound types for Java. In *OOPSLA'98: Proceedings of the 13th ACM SIGPLAN conference on Object-Oriented Programming, Systems, Languages, and Applications*, pages 362–373, New York, NY, USA, 1998. ACM Press.
10. Luca Cardelli. *The Handbook of Computer Science and Engineering*, chapter 103, Type Systems, pages 2208–2236. CRC Press, Boca Raton, FL, 1997.
11. John Cheesman and John Daniels. *UML components: a simple process for specifying component-based software*. Addison-Wesley Longman Publishing Co., Inc., Boston, MA, USA, 2000.
12. Michael Eichberg. Mda and programming languages. In *Workshop on Generative Techniques in the context of Model Driven Architecture (OOPSLA '02)*, 2002.
13. Patrick Th. Eugster, Pascal A. Felber, Rachid Guerraoui, and Anne-Marie Kermarrec. The many faces of publish/subscribe. *ACM Comput. Surv.*, 35(2):114–131, 2003.
14. Houssam Fakih, Noury Bouraqadi, and Laurence Duchien. Aspects and software components: A case study of the FRACTAL component model. In Minhuan Huang, Hong Mei, and Jianjun Zhao, editors, *International Workshop on Aspect-Oriented Software Development (WAOSD 2004)*, September 2004.
15. FracTalk. Fractal Components in Smalltalk http://csl.ensm-douai.fr/FracTalk.
16. Peter H. Fröhlich, Andreas Gal, and Michael Franz. Supporting software composition at the programming-language level. *Science of Computer Programming, Special Issue on New Software Composition Concept*, 56(1-2):41–57, April 2005.
17. Erich Gamma, Richard Helm, Ralph Johnson, and John Vlissides. *Design Patterns: Elements of Reusable Object-Oriented Software*. Addison Wesley, March 1995.
18. David Garlan and Mary Shaw. An introduction to software architecture. In V. Ambriola and G. Tortora, editors, *Advances in Software Engineering and Knowledge Engineering*, pages 1–39, Singapore, 1993. World Scientific Publishing Company.

19. Adele Goldberg and David Robson. *Smalltalk-80: The Language.* Addison-Wesley Longman Publishing Co., Inc., Boston, MA, USA, 1989.
20. Bernhard Gröne, Andreas Knöpfel, and Peter Tabeling. Component vs. component: Why we need more than one definition. In *ECBS*, pages 550–552. IEEE Computer Society, 2005.
21. Object Management Group. Uml 2.0 superstructure specification. Technical report, Object Management Group, 2004.
22. Graham Hamilton. JavaBeans. API Specification, Sun Microsystems, July 1997. Version 1.01.
23. George T. Heineman and William T. Councill, editors. *Component-based software engineering: putting the pieces together.* Addison-Wesley Longman Publishing Co., Inc., Boston, MA, USA, 2001.
24. Dan Ingalls, Ted Kaehler, John Maloney, Scott Wallace, and Alan Kay. Back to the future: the story of Squeak, a practical Smalltalk written in itself. In *OOPSLA '97: Proceedings of the 12th ACM SIGPLAN conference on Object-oriented programming, systems, languages, and applications*, pages 318–326, New York, NY, USA, 1997. ACM Press.
25. Gregor Kiczales, Erik Hilsdale, Jim Hugunin, Mik Kersten, Jeffrey Palm, and William G. Griswold. An Overview of AspectJ. In Jørgen Lindskov Knudsen, editor, *ECOOP*, volume 2072 of *Lecture Notes in Computer Science*, pages 327–353. Springer, 2001.
26. Gregor Kiczales, John Lamping, Anurag Mendhekar, Chris Maeda, Cristina Lopes, Jean-Marc Loingtier, and John Irwin. Aspect-oriented programming. In Mehmet Akşit and Satoshi Matsuoka, editors, *11th Europeen Conf. Object-Oriented Programming*, volume 1241 of *LNCS*, pages 220–242. Springer Verlag, 1997.
27. Glenn E. Krasner and Stephen T. Pope. A cookbook for using the model-view-controller user interface paradigm in smalltalk-80. In *Journal of Object-Oriented Programming*, volume 1, pages 26–49, Août-Septembre 1988.
28. Simple Component Language. http://www.lirmm.fr/~fabresse/scl/.
29. Y. Liu and H. C. Cunningham. Boxscript: A component-oriented language for teaching. In *43rd ACM-Southeast Conference*, volume 1, pages 349–354, March 2005.
30. Raphaël Marvie. Picolo: A simple python framework for introducing component principles. In *Euro Python Conference 2005*, Göteborg, Sweden, june 2005.
31. M. D. McIlroy. Mass produced software components. In P. Naur and B. Randell, editors, *Proceedings, NATO Conference on Software Engineering*, Garmisch, Germany, October 1968.
32. Nenad Medvidovic and Richard N. Taylor. A classification and comparison framework for software architecture description languages. *Software Engineering*, 26(1):70–93, 2000.
33. Nikunj R. Mehta, Nenad Medvidovic, and Sandeep Phadke. Towards a taxonomy of software connectors. In *ICSE '00: Proceedings of the 22nd international conference on Software engineering*, pages 178–187, New York, NY, USA, 2000. ACM Press.
34. Microsoft. DCOM technical overview. Microsoft Windows NT Server white paper, Microsoft Corporation, 1996.
35. M. Minsky. A Framework for Representing Knowledge. In P. Winston, editor, *The Psychology of Computer Vision*, pages 211–281. mgh, ny, 1975.
36. Oscar Nierstrasz and Laurent Dami. Component-oriented software technology. In Oscar Nierstrasz and Dennis Tsichritzis, editors, *Object-Oriented Software Composition*, pages 3–28. Prentice-Hall, 1995.

37. Object Management Group. *Model Driven Architecture*, 2003. *http://www.omg. org/mda*.
38. D. L. Parnas. On the criteria to be used in decomposing systems into modules. *Comm. ACM*, 15(12):1053–1058, December 1972.
39. N. Pessemier, L. Seinturier, L. Duchien, and T. Coupaye. A model for developing component-based and aspect-oriented systems. In *Proceedings of the 5th International Symposium on Software Composition (SC'06)*, volume 4089 of *Lecture Notes in Computer Science*. Springer, March 2006.
40. Frantisek Plasil and Stanislav Visnovsky. Behavior protocols for software components. *IEEE Trans. Softw. Eng.*, 28(11):1056–1076, 2002.
41. Johannes Sametinger. *Software engineering with reusable components*. Springer-Verlag New York, Inc., New York, NY, USA, 1997.
42. João Costa Seco and Luís Caires. A basic model of typed components. *Lecture Notes in Computer Science*, 1850:108–129, 2000.
43. Mary Shaw. Procedure calls are the assembly language of software interconnection: Connectors deserve first-class status. In *ICSE '93: Selected papers from the Workshop on Studies of Software Design*, pages 17–32, London, UK, 1996. Springer-Verlag.
44. Davy Suvée, Wim Vanderperren, and Viviane Jonckers. Jasco: an aspect-oriented approach tailored for component based software development. In *AOSD '03: Proceedings of the 2nd international conference on Aspect-oriented software development*, pages 21–29, New York, NY, USA, 2003. ACM Press.
45. C. Szyperski. *Component Software: Beyond Object-Oriented Programming (2nd Edition)*. Addison-Wesley, 2002.
46. Rob C. van Ommering. Koala, a component model for consumer electronics product software. In Frank van der Linden, editor, *ESPRIT ARES Workshop*, volume 1429 of *Lecture Notes in Computer Science*, pages 76–86. Springer, 1998.
47. Matthias Zenger. Type-safe prototype-based component evolution. In *Proceedings of the European Conference on Object-Oriented Programming*, Malaga, Spain, June 2002.
48. Matthias Zenger. Keris: evolving software with extensible modules: Research articles. *J. Softw. Maint. Evol.*, 17(5):333–362, 2005.

Let's Modularize the Data Model Specifications of the ObjectLens in VisualWorks/Smalltalk

Michael Prasse

Collogia Unternehmungsberatung AG,
Ubierring 11, D-50678 Köln, Germany
michael.prasse@collogia.de

Abstract. The ObjectLens framework of VisualWorks maps objects to tables. This mapping is described in a data mapping model, which itself is specified in one dataModelSpec method. This method is monolithic and defines the whole data model of an application. This is a suitable approach to start with. However, when the business area extends to a set of similar applications, like a software product family, each of these applications needs its own data model specification. All specifications of the product family would be quite similar but there is no appropriate reuse-mechanism, which could be used. Consequently, the monolithic design specifications lead to a high degree of redundancy, which complicates software development and maintenance. Therefore, this paper describes an approach, which leads to a separation of the monolithic data model specifications. The main idea is to define the mappings of each class in the class itself using inheritance and generate the whole specification from a list of single class data models. In this way, declarative and generative programming techniques are combined.

Keywords: ObjectLens, Smalltalk, VisualWorks, Design Pattern, Software Product Families, OR-Mapping, Generative Programming.

1 Introduction

Since 1997 our software engineering group develops applications in the domain of pension schemes with VisualWorks/Smalltalk. At the beginning this software was specified for one customer. In the course of time the number of customers and the application domains grew. Today we support more than 20 customers and all kinds of pension schemes in Germany including long-term accounts of employees. The system architecture is extended from a fat client architecture to an application service provider architecture including a web application server, which is also built in VisualWorks.

To reduce software engineering costs we organized our applications as a product family. There is a single source base for all applications improving reuse of existing modules. The core is organized as a framework including common GUI-standards, common domain specific models, database access layers and standard management and administration modules. The applications extend this core by defining new specific modules using object-oriented techniques like inheritance, object composition and meta programming.

W. De Meuter (Ed.): ISC 2006, LNCS 4406, pp. 111–133, 2007.

But there is one area where we could not achieve a high degree of reuse directly. This is how object-relational mappings are defined in the ObjectLens framework, which is the heart of the data base access layer. In the ObjectLens, the object-relational mappings are described in one monolithic specification. We need a specific object-relational mapping for each application. All these specifications have common parts. Defining a new specification starts with copying a suitable specification and changing it. This copy-paste approach leads to a high level of redundancy and makes data model changes of common parts more difficult because many specifications have to be updated. In this paper we want to describe a more sophisticated solution solving these problems.

The presented solution is a pragmatic one. The first aim was to solve the redundancy and maintenance problem concerning the data model specifications. It was not our goal to do extensive academic research on object-relational mapping or to develop a new object-relational mapping framework. For example, there is no opportunity to exchange the base object relational mapping of our applications. The costs and time are in no relation to the expected benefits. For these reasons our solution has to be integrated in the existing ObjectLens. Of course to achieve our primary aim of improving the data model specifications we used an engineering approach including analysis, design, risk management, testing and stepwise deployment in production.

The article is structured as following. First the ObjectLens framework of Visual-Works is introduced. Then the data model specifications of the ObjectLens and their disadvantages for our product line approach are discussed in detail. Afterwards we present our solution and its integration in the ObjectLens framework. In the next section we describe the generation of our new data model specification parts from the old specifications and how we solve specification conflicts. The conclusion summarizes our experiences.

2 ObjectLens Framework

The ObjectLens Framework is an integrated part of VisualWorks since Version 2.0 from 1994 ([5], [19]). The major concepts of the ObjectLens have not changed since then. It is an early developed access framework for mapping objects to relational database tables. It is comparable to other early OR-mapping tools from this time like TOPLink by The Object People Inc., now Oracle, Polar by IBL Ingenieurbüro Letters GmbH, Arcus Relational Database Access Layers by sd&m, MicroDoc Persistence Framework by MicoDoc GmbH or Crossing Chasms Pattern Language by Kyle Brown ([4], [14], [15], [18], [23])[1].

In the next subsections, we describe the architecture, the object mapping to tables and the programming metaphor of the ObjectLens.

2.1 Architecture

The ObjectLens Framework consists of four modules, which are described abstractly in Figure 1. The declaration module defines the specifications to describe the data

---

[1] We enumerate only approaches which were introduced at the same time like the ObjectLens. Therefore, GLORP (Smalltalk), JDO (Java) or Hibernate (Java, .NET) are not considered ([3], [16], [22]).

model in a logical way. This module contains classes for describing the data model and the data model specification. The data model is a set of objects and defines data structure types, variables, types, and foreign key relationships. The data model specifications are a declarative way to define this data model. Furthermore, it uses the database module, which describes database tables and columns, to specify the mapping to the logical database design. Together, both modules describe the logical database design and mapping. There are also tools like the data modeler and the mapping tool, which allow to specify the data model specifications tool based. Furthermore, you can generate or adapt the logical database structure from a data model specification automatically. This process is called "*check with database*".

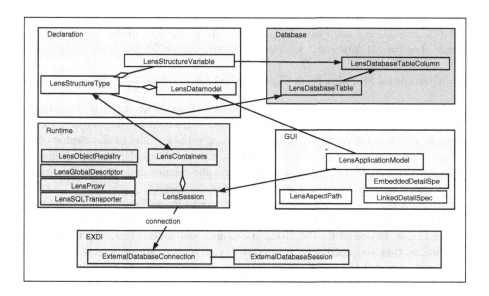

Fig. 1. Technical Architecture

The next module is the runtime engine. It defines the infrastructure, which is required for mapping objects to table rows and vice versa at runtime. It contains classes for row containers, caching, proxies, and SQL queries. Furthermore, it defines a lens session, which controls the access to the persistent objects. This module supports a seamless integration of SQL queries into Smalltalk and reduces the impedance mismatch ([8]).

The last module defines GUI widgets for viewing and editing persistent objects. These widgets are integrated seamlessly into the GUI framework of VisualWorks. Transient and persistent objects can therefore be represented in the same way. It defines also aspect paths, which allow connections between the object aspects and the visual components via the ValueModel-pattern ([2], [6], [13], [24]).

The ObjectLens itself is based on the EXDI framework (external database interface), which provides a low level access to database programming. The EXDI provides a set of abstract protocols to establish a connection to the database server, to prepare and execute SQL queries, to obtain the results, and to disconnect from the server. It supports also flat or non-nested database transactions with begin, commit, and rollback.

The EXDI is an abstract framework. It provides the general implementation, but it does not provide direct support for any particular database. Database Connect extensions are available to provide connectivity to specific databases. Our software engineering group uses database connections for Oracle, DB2, and PostgreSQL. The original ObjectLens framework was build for Oracle and later Sybase. Today we use extensions, which allow to support DB2 and PostgreSQL. Therefore, we can run our applications with different RDBMS without changing any code. The data models of DB2 and PostgreSQL are automatically generated from the data model specification of Oracle. The current database is selected by a configuration file.

2.2 Conceptual Mapping from Classes to Tables

The conceptual mapping from classes to tables of the ObjectLens is described in Table 1. The ObjectLens uses a simple mapping, which directly maps object-oriented concepts to relational concepts. Classes, instance variables, and monomorphic object references are mapped directly to tables and columns. 1:N and N:M relationships can be modeled by auxiliary classes, which express the relationships or by explicit queries, which select all objects that are connected to the object.

Unfortunately, the ObjectLens has only restricted support for inheritance and polymorphism. Each class is always unambiguously mapped to one table. You cannot map several classes to one table. Therefore, you cannot map a class hierarchy to one table. That means that you need several queries if you want to select objects of different subclasses. Alternatively, you can replace inheritance by object composition but this can lead to a complicated class design.

For example, you could use a class A for the queries, which has no subclasses. If class A is used for queries, then only one query is needed to access all objects. The class A has a reference to the root class B of a class hierarchy. This reference is mapped by an untyped object reference so that objects of A can point to objects of subclasses of B. The cost of this design is the separation of one domain entity in two subparts.

Foreign key relationships can only be mapped for monomorphic instance variables. That means such a variable can only hold objects from one class. If you want to use polymorphic variables, which can reference to objects from different classes, you have to build untyped relationships. However, in this case you have to manage the access itself.

2.3 Programming Metaphor

The ObjectLens uses explicit persistency. The metaphor of persistency of the Object-Lens is the persistent container or collection. It uses no persistency by reachability,

Table 1. Object Relational Mapping of the ObjectLens

Mapping Support	Concept	Mapping
	calculus level (static semantics)[2]	Φ: object calculus $\rightarrow$ relational calculus
directly	class level	$\Phi_{classes}$: classes $\rightarrow$ tables Each class is unambiguously mapped to one table. In one data model, no table can be mapped to different classes. This restriction holds because the classID of objects is not stored in the tables. Therefore, you cannot map inheritance or polymorphism by storing objects of different classes (subclasses) in the same table.
directly	instance variable level	$\Phi_{instance\ variables}$: variables $\rightarrow$ columns
	instance variables with simple data types	Instance variables with simple data types can be mapped directly to one column.
	instance variables with monomorphic object references (1:1 relationship)	Instance variables that hold object references map to a set of columns, which holds the primary key of this object. This set of columns realizes a foreign key relationship.
indirectly	1:n and n:m relationships	There is no direct representation. Additional tables in the database and select-statements of the ObjectLens can implement these relationships.[3]
no support	inheritance	There is no direct representation. Each subclass is mapped to its own table. Each table contains all instance variables of the class including inherited variables.
no support	polymorphism	Polymorphism for object references is not supported by the ObjectLens. We developed an extension, which allows to support untyped object references. For such references, the foreign key consists of the pair (classID, objectID).

---

[2] For an introduction to relational databases and the relational calculus see [9] or [10]. For an introduction to object calculi and object-oriented concepts see [1], [17] or [20].

[3] ObjectLens select-statements are Smalltalk statements, which are automatically transformed in SQL queries by the ObjectLens.

where all objects, which are reachable from a persistent root object are persistent, or persistent classes, where all objects of the class are automatically persistent.

The ObjectLens is interpreted as a collection. To make an object persistent, it is simply added to the lens session. To remove an object from the database, it is simple removed from the lens session. The syntax is comparable to theirs of collections:

- to make an object persistent: *aLensSession add: anObject*
- to remove an object from the database: *aLensSession remove: anObject*

For all objects, which are included in the lens session, changes are automatically detected. Each state change of such an object leads to an *isDirty*-registration. This *isDirty*-mechanism is integrated in the setter methods of all instance variables by using the private method *update:to:* of the ObjectLens. Each state change using a setter method is therefore detected. To reduce coding errors, the getter and setter methods for instance variables can be automatically generated.

The ObjectLens supports flat transactions. Therefore, all updates, which occur in a transaction, are written either together in the database (commit) or are rejected (rollback). Furthermore, you can use the ObjectLens without transactions. In this case changes are immediately written into the database.

Database queries can also be written in Smalltalk. The syntax is comparable to the method *select* of collections. The base for queries is the class *LensQuery*. Where-clauses are expressed as block closures like in the collection methods *do:*, *select:* or *detect:*. Figure 2 shows an example of a select-statement from our domain.

```
readEmployees: anEmployer in: anApplication
    ^anApplication
        selectOnContainer: self container
            whereBlock: [:each | each employer = anEmployer & each isCurrent]
```

Fig. 2. Select-statement in Smalltalk

The result list of a query is automatically transformed into corresponding objects. Object references are expressed as lens proxies. If a proxy is accessed it is automatically resolved by the corresponding object. An object cache ensures referential integrity. All these mechanisms help to abstract from the relational persistent mechanism and the database access in the ObjectLens. In most cases, Smalltalk syntax can be used for persistent objects, which reduces the impedance mismatch.

The ObjectLens supports multiple lens sessions. An application can use several lens sessions to access different databases simultaneously. However, the ObjectLens has no multi-process ability. It is impossible to access one lens session from different threads or processes. The implementation of the ObjectLens uses singletons for building the SQL-requests and is therefore not thread safe.

One further disadvantage is the bad performance by mass queries, if object references are resolved by single queries. This is a typical trade-off of object references and object navigation. Object navigation is fast, but a query over a set of such objects needs additional queries for each object in the set. You can influence this by using explicit select statements for mass queries.

2.4 Summary

The ObjectLens together with the EXDI framework and the specific Database Connect extensions provides support for the most relevant aspects of building database applications. This includes the declaration of the mappings, the creation and adaptation of the database tables, the low level database access, the creation of user interfaces for persistent objects and the runtime support with storing objects into the database, retrieving objects from the database and querying the database, which Smalltalk queries, which are translated into SQL.

The ObjectLens provides also a simple mapping from object-oriented concepts to relational concepts. Inheritance and polymorphism are not directly supported. Nevertheless, there are ways to achieve both.

In the most cases you can think about the ObjectLens as a persistent collection. To make an object persistent, you add it. To remove an object from the database, you remove it from the Lens. To select an object from the database, you send a select statement to the Lens. The technical aspects like transactions, proxies, posting updates, and translating queries into SQL are done by the ObjectLens.

Summarizing, the ObjectLens is an object-oriented access layer to relational databases. Its advantages are:

- a seamless integration in VisualWorks
- good support access by navigation and single queries
- the generation of the database scheme
- RDBMS-abstraction (Oracle, Sybase, DB2, ODBC, (PostgreSQL))
- GUI-support
- the support of multiple lens sessions
- graphical modeling tools for describing and generating data models

Its disadvantages are:

- only rudimentary support of inheritance and polymorphism
- bad performance by mass queries
- no multiprocessor ability

3 Data Model Specification

After introducing the ObjectLens let us look now at the data model specifications, which describe the mapping for one application. In the next subsections, we describe the structure of the *dataModelSpec*, the problems of maintenance and first solutions.

3.1 Conceptualization

The *datamodelSpec* is a declarative description of a lens data model. It is coded as a literal array (*LiteralArray*). A literal array is an array of arrays of literals. It is recursively defined. Literal arrays are widely used in VisualWorks. Its most prominent use in VisualWorks is the *windowSpec* of the GUI-Framework. All windows, which use the VisualWorks framework, are declarative described by literal arrays. Another example is the specification of diagrams by the Advance UML modeling tool of VisualWorks, which uses *ad2diagram* methods ([6], [13]).

To encode a lens data model, you use the method *literalArrayEncoding*. To decode a lens data model, you use the method *fromLiteralArrayEncoding:*.

- encoding: *aLensDataModel literalArrayEncoding* returns a literal array suitable for reconstituting the receiver.
- decoding: *LensDataModel fromLiteralArrayEncoding: anArray* creates a lens data model from the array encoding.
- *LensDataModel fromLiteralArrayEncoding: (aLensDataModel literalArrayEncoding)* returns a lens data model, which is equal to *aLensDataModel*.

If you apply the methods *literalArrayEncoding* and *fromLiteralArrayEncoding:* alternately then you can switch between the data model level and the data model specification level. This means, that you can choose the language level for the specification of the data model specifications.

Figure 3 shows the general structure of a literal array and of a *dataModelSpec* method. A literal array consists of two central parts: a class and a set of (aspect, value) pairs. The class determines the kind of object, which the literal array describes. The (aspect, value) pairs describe the state of the object. Usually the aspect is a method selector and the value is the argument. The receiver of the object is the recently constructed object. In general, the construction process uses therefore a set of method sends of the form '<object> <aspect> <value>'. The value itself can be encoded as a literal array leading to nested encodings.

The general structure of a lens literal array is also described by Figure 3[4]. The first aspect defines the database context. The second aspect describes the containing structure types. This is the most important aspect of the description because a lens data model is mostly a set of structure types. The next two aspects describe policies. The validity aspect determines the definition state of the data model.

The literal array of a lens structure type determines the class of the structure type, the variables of the structure type and the table. The literal array of a lens structure variable determines name, mapping, and column of the variable. The <value> for the aspect *#structureTypes:* is a collection of structure types and the <value> of the aspect *#setVariables:* is a collection of structure variables.

Figure 4 shows the beginning of an existing *dataModelSpec* method, which is part of our system. As shown in Figure 3 the structure types are described as literal arrays. The definition database is an *Oracle7Context* with user name 'lens' and database 'lensDB'. The example shows the beginning of the specification of the lens structure type *COLAdresse*. A lens structure type itself consists of a set of lens structure variables. In the example, the definition for the variable 'dependents' is shown. This is an unmapped (transient) variable. The *datamodelSpec* can specify persistent variables, which are mapped, and transient variables, which are unmapped. Each lens structure

---

[4] The literal array is not described in all details. Only the most important aspects are shown.

```
literal array
    ^#(<Class>
        <aspect> <value> <aspect> <value> <aspect> <value> ...)

lens literal array
    ^#(#{Lens.LensDataModel}
        #setDatabaseContext: #(...)
        #structureTypes: #(
                #(#{Lens.LensStructureType}
                        #memberClass: <memberClass>
                        #setVariables: #(
                            #(#{Lens.LensStructureVariable}
                                #name: 'angelegtAm'
                                #column: <Database Column>
                                #privateIsMapped: true )
                            ...)
                        #table: <Database Table> )
                ...)
        #lensPolicyName: #Mixed
        #lensTransactionPolicyName: #PessimisticRR
        #validity: #installed )
```

Fig. 3. Structure of Literal Arrays and Lens Literal Arrays

type, which is used as a type of a lens structure variable, has to be defined in the *data-ModelSpec*. This is a completeness constraint to the specification.

3.2   Maintenance Problems

The maintenance problems, which we identified by using the ObjectLens, can be classified into two groups. The first group contains problems, which result from the poor support of inheritance by the ObjectLens. In the second group are problems, which result from the move to a product family with different *datamodelSpecs*. The origin of both problem groups is redundancy.

3.2.1   Class Hierarchy Problems
The lens structure type of a class defines all instance variables of a class including in-herited variables. This is necessary because the corresponding table has to store all variables of the objects. Therefore, in each subclass of a class all instance variables of that class have to be defined once again. There is no single source principle for the specification of the mapping of instance variables.

These multiple definitions lead to some maintenance problems. If a new subclass is added to a *dataModelSpec* using the lens data modeler, the mappings of the inherited

```
dataModelSpec
   "LensEditor new openOnClass: self andSelector: #dataModelSpec"
   <resource: #dataModel>
   ^#(#{Lens.LensDataModel}
      #setDatabaseContext:
      #(#{Oracle7Context}
         #username: 'lens'
         #environment: 'lensDB' )
      #structureTypes: #(
         #(#{Lens.LensStructureType}
            #memberClass: #{COLAdresse}
            #setVariables: #(
               #(#{Lens.LensStructureVariable}
                  #name: 'dependents'
                  #setValueType: #Object
                  #generatesAccessor: false
                  #generatesMutator: false
                  #privateIsMapped: false ) ...
```

Fig. 4. Example dataModelSpec

instance variables are not taken over. They have to be specified again, what is cumbersome and error prone. If a new variable is added to a superclass then all lens structure types of the subclasses have to be changed. The renaming of an instance variable of a superclass requires analogous adaptations. The same instance variable can be mapped variously to the database in different subclasses. In some situations, this flexibility could be an advantage. More often, different mappings are unwanted and only the result of missed adaptations. For example the property gender of a person is mapped to {'m','f'} in some subclasses and to a boolean in other subclasses of the same data model.

The same situation occurs if the superclass of a class is changed. In this case all instances variables of the old superclass have to be removed from the specification and all instance variables of the new superclass have to be added with the correct mapping. Figure 5 shows an example. The superclass of the class *AtzBeleg* is changed from *ZEBeleg* to *BelegMitRechtskreis*. The red-colored variables are changed. They need therefore a new mapping. If you remember that this is information of the superclass you understand that each change in the class hierarchy inflicts subclasses directly.

3.2.2 Multiple DatamodelSpec Problems

One monolithic *datamodelSpec* is used to describe the data model of an application. The data model has to contain all entity classes of the application. When we switched

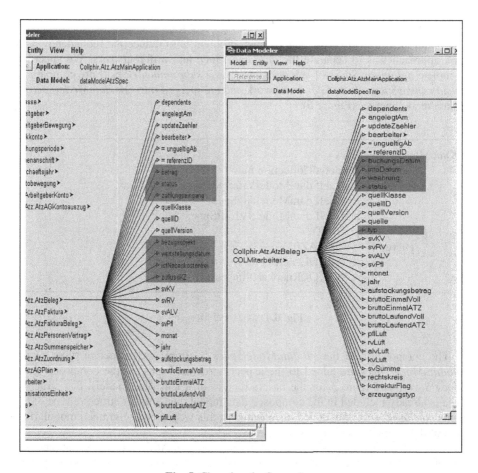

Fig. 5. Changing the Superclass

from one application to a product family, we had suddenly to deal with multiple *data-modelSpecs*. Common shared core modules and domain specific modules characterize the product family. If we start a new project for a customer in the domain context, we often copy and paste an existing *dataModelSpec* of an old project. Then this *data-modelSpec* is adapted to the new requirements.

Concerning the common core modules, all our *dataModelSpec* have overlapping parts. So changing the mapping of a superclass in a core module results not only in modifications of the subclasses in one *datamodelSpec*, but also in all the other *data-modelSpecs*. Extending a core module by a new persistent class requires again modifications to all *datamodelSpec*. If these changes are not maintained to all applications then inconsistencies and different mappings may arise.

The origin of all these problems is the redundant specification of instance variable mappings in subclasses and *datamodelSpecs*. There is no single source principle for specifications of the ObjectLens.

3.3 The DataModelMerger as a First Solution Approach

The main idea to resolve the maintenance problem is to reduce the redundancy. Our first approach was to separate the *datamodelSpec* into different parts. We specified complete *datamodelSpecs* of sub domains. These *subdatamodelSpecs* are comparable to *subcanvasSpecs* of the GUI framework and are merged into one *dataModelSpec* by a data model merger (Figure 6).

```
DataModelMerger new
        mergeAll: (OrderedCollection new
                add: self dataModelVifaSpec;
                add: self dataModelAtzSpec;
                add: self dataModelSVLuftSpec;
                yourself)
        ignore: #( #( #COLAZ03)
                #(#COLAZRR)
                #(#COLRueckzahlungssatz) )
```

Fig. 6. Data Model Merger

The composition of the *subdataModelSpecs* is simple. All structure types of the *subdataModelSpecs* are added to the aspect 'structureTypes' of the composed *dataModelSpec* (see Figure 3 for the base structure of a lens data model). If a structure type is already included in the composed data model then another structure type of the same *memberClass* is not added once again. In this way, a coarse-grained modularization of the ObjectLens is achieved.

Nevertheless, this approach remains unsatisfactorily. At first, it solves not the class hierarchy problems. At second, the domain *subdataModelSpecs* are still too extensive. Each *subdataModelSpec* has to be complete with regard to all used lens structure types. Therefore, there are common classes like *Employee*, *Employer*, or *Person*, which are included in all *subdataModelSpecs*. At third, the *subdataModelSpecs* includes often classes, which are not needed. Some of these classes can be removed from the data model by including these into the ignore set.

3.4 Summary

In conclusion, the *dataModelSpec* is a declarative description of a data model. It is coded as a literal array. Unfortunately, the *dataModelSpec* is a monolithic definition, which has only limited support for inheritance. Therefore, a number of problems occur during defining and maintaining such data model specifications. The origin of all these problems is the redundant specification of instance variable mappings in subclasses and *datamodelSpecs*. This redundant definition leads to problems when adding or changing variables of a superclass, when adding a new subclass or when changing the superclass. Specification conflicts can occur if the same variable is mapped differently in different subclasses. The main idea to resolve these maintenance problems is to reduce the redundancy.

4   Modularization of the ObjectLens

Up to now, we introduced the ObjectLens and described their relational database mapping and associated disadvantages. Now we explain our approach to overcome these problems in the following sections. At first, we describe the general ideas and aims of the solution. Then we point out the definitions of the lens mapping for the single domain classes. After that, we demonstrate the integration of the mappings of the single domain classes into one data model of the lens application. Then we explain the migration of our old data models into the modular data models. At the end, we show the integration of our approach into the common database developer tools of VisualWorks.

4.1   General Ideas and Goals

The general aspects of our solution are modularization and the use of inheritance. If you remember, the lack of inheritance and the monolithic design of the data model specifications of the ObjectLens are the origin of redundancy and the related problems. We decided to break up the monolithic specification in several pieces with each piece describing the mapping of one class[5]. Furthermore, we use inheritance if we want to describe the object relational mapping for one class. Therefore, only the parts of a class without inherited variables have to be considered. The data model specification of a lens application is defined by the data model specifications of the contained set of classes. That means that the single class data specifications are the pieces from which the whole data model specification is constructed. The result is a normal, but generated monolithic data model specification of the ObjectLens. Therefore, we changed only the definition and construction process of the data model specifications.

This approach gives us the desired advantages. We achieve a better adaptation, a unification of the data representation of different applications in the product family and the use of inheritance. In some way, we look at the *datamodelSpec* as one aspect of the class and organize this aspect by the class itself. The modularization of the *datamodelSpec* simplifies the maintenance efforts significantly. Instead of changing a central monolithic definition, we change only the modular definitions of the concerned classes.

Therefore, our solution consists of four parts. We store the mappings in the domain classes. We construct automatically the *datamodelSpec* from these mapping fragments. We support the common development tools. We support the migration of our existing data model specifications.

4.2   Data Model Mappings of Classes

The data model specification of a class defines the corresponding lens structure type, whereby definitions of inherited variables are obtained from the superclasses. The definition of one class uses the definition of the superclass. Variables are described as lens structure variables (remember Figure 3). The lens structure type of a single class can easily be integrated in the aggregated data model specification.

---

[5]   This approach is comparable to instVarMaps of GemStone. You can control instance variable mappings between GemStone and your client Smalltalk by using these methods ([11]).

---

dataModelDefinitionSpec
  " You should not override this message. "
  ^ self dataModelDefinition literalArrayEncoding

dataModelDefinition
  " You should not override this message.
  You can adapt primDataModelDefinition"

  | type |
  type := self primDataModelDefinition.
  self primLocalDataModelDefinitionChanges: type.
  type variables: (List withAll: type variables).
  type resolveStandalone.
  ^type

Fig. 7. Public Protocol for Class Data Model Definitions

Figure 7 shows the public protocol for defining the data models of a class. This definition uses the template method pattern like the methods *printString* and *prinOn*: ([2], [12]). The method *dataModelDefinition* provides an abstract implementation, which should be used by all classes. The method *dataModelDefinition* should not be overridden. First, the method *primDataModelDefinition* is called, which provides the standard implementation. After that, the method *primLocalDataModelDefinitionChanges*: is called. This method gives each class the opportunity to override the inherited definitions. Whereas the method *primDataModelDefinition* will usually be automatically generated, the method *primLocalDataModelDefinitionChanges* is created by hand and describes changes, which should not be overridden by further generation steps. The persistent classes of our product family are subclasses of *COLPersistentModel*. Therefore, we define the template methods for defining the lens structure types in this class in the method protocol '*lens data model specs*'.

Figure 8 shows the basis hook method of the class *COLPersistentModel* and a further example. It also displays the usual way in which a lens structure type is defined. We use the *LensMetaData* classes directly. At first, we create an object of class *LensStructureType*. After that, the member class and the table are set up. The other example demonstrates the definition of structure variables of the persistent instance variables. Here we use the literal encodings. The decision to use literal encodings for variables is a pragmatic one. We want to simplify the migration process of our existing *dataModelSpecs* and we want to use the facilities of the ObjectLens for generating lens encodings. Variables with simple data types are directly included in the method. Instance variables for object references (foreign key relationships) are defined in separate

---

COLPersistentModel>>primDataModelDefinition
"hook method"

| type |
type := LensStructureType new.
type memberClass: self.
type table: ((Oracle7Table new) name: self name; owner: 'COLBAV').
type idGeneratorType: #userDefinedId.
^type

primDataModelDefinition
| type |
type := super primDataModelDefinition.

type variables add: #(#{Lens.LensStructureVariable} #name: 'name'
#setValueType: #String #fieldType: #String #column: #(#{Oracle7TableColumn}
#name: 'name' #dataType: 'varchar2' #maxColumnConstraint: 100)
#generatesAccessor: false #generatesMutator: false #privateIsMapped: true)
decodeAsLiteralArray.

self addSummenspeicherVariableIn: type.

type idVariable: #('ungueltigAb' 'referenzID') .
type table name: 'kontoZuordnung' .

^type

Fig. 8. Hook Method primDataModelDefinition

methods, because our objects use two-dimensional primary keys and therefore the corresponding literal encodings are more complex. At the end, primary key and table name are defined[6].

Figure 9 shows an example for the hook method *primLocalDataModelDefinitionChanges:*, which can be used for adapting inherited properties. In the example, the variable *speicherBeleg* gets a new type. On the database the variable *speicherbeleg* is mapped as a foreign key relationship to the table of *AtzSummenspeicherBeleg*. This allows the simulation of covariant instance variable redefinitions[7].

The hook methods *primDataModelDefinition* and *primLocalDataModelDefinitionChanges* are used to define a lens structure type of a class. The template methods *dataModelDefinition* and *dataModelDefinitionSpec* are the public interface. They are used for integrating the class fragments into the whole data model specification.

---

[6] In general the primary key is taken from the superclass and the table name is set to the name of the class.

[7] For an explanation of the co- and contravariance issue of object-orientation see [1], [7], [20].

```
primLocalDataModelDefinitionChanges:type
    | var |
    super primLocalDataModelDefinitionChanges:type.
    (type variableNamed: 'speicherBeleg')
                setValueType: #AtzSummenspeicherBeleg
```

Fig. 9. Hook Method primLocalDataModelDefinitionChanges

4.3 LensApplication datamodelSpec

Now we consider the application side. Like we showed above, the old data model specification describes the data models of the persistent classes of an application. Therefore, we need to define the set of classes, which belong to the data model. This is
done by the class method *dataModelClasses*. The set has to include all classes, which
are referred in the data model (transient closure), otherwise the data model specification cannot be created. We choose this decision to make the declaration explicit.
There are methods, which can calculate the transient closure of a set of classes so that
the resulting data model is complete.

The second step is the generation of the whole data model specification from the
data model classes. We describe this construction top down. The top method is the
method *dataModelSpecGenerated* (Figure 10). In this method, an object of *Lens-
DataModel* is created from the specifications of the data model classes. This is done
by the code fragment *"self dataModelSpecForStructureTypeSpecs: self dataModel-
StructureTypeSpecs"*. The method *adaptDataModel* is a further hook method, which
permits adaptations, which are only valid for this special application. In the last step,
the data model is compiled and the method returns the literal encoding of the data
model. This method is quite short in contrast to our old *dataModelSpecs* with more
than 15000 LOC of formatted code. These are 970 pages of formatted text or 250
pages of unformatted text without any line feed.

```
dataModelSpecGenerated
    | ldm |
    (ldm := LensDataModel new)
        application: self;
        fromLiteralArrayEncoding: (self dataModelSpecForStructureTypeSpecs:
                                        self dataModelStructureTypeSpecs).
    self adaptDataModel: ldm.
    ldm compile.
    ^ldm literalArrayEncoding
```

Fig. 10. LensMainApplication class >> dataModelSpecGenerated (Part 1)

Now we consider the method *dataModelSpecForStructureTypeSpecs* and its implementation (Figure 11). The method returns the data model specifications of the data model classes. The method *dataModelStructureTypeSpecsFor:* shows the connection to the data model specifications of the classes. For each class in the set of data model classes the corresponding literal encoding is collected.

---

dataModelStructureTypeSpecs
   ^ self dataModelStructureTypeSpecsFor: self dataModelClasses

dataModelStructureTypeSpecsFor: classColl
   ^ (classColl collect:[:cl | cl dataModelDefinitionSpec]) asArray

---

Fig. 11. Methods dataModelStructureTypeSpecs and dataModelStructureTypeSpecsFor: (Part 2)

The last step concerns the implementation of the method *dataModelSpecForStructureTypeSpecs* (Figure 12). The array of data model specification literal encodings for the data model classes is inserted in the data model template. The method *dataModelTemplate* provides the general template of the lens data model encoding (see also Figure 3). The array of structure types is put at position 5.

These few methods describe the generation of the data model specification of the application from the specification fragments of the data model classes. The two central aspects are the determination of the set of data classes and the knowledge that for the generation of the data model specification of the application only the specifications of the lens structure types have to be inserted.

---

dataModelSpecForStructureTypeSpecs: aColl
   | res |
   res := self dataModelTemplate copy.
   res at: 5 put: aColl.
   ^res

dataModelTemplate
   ^#(#{Lens.LensDataModel}
      #setDatabaseContext:
      #(#{Oracle7Context} ...)
      #structureTypes: #()
      #lensPolicyName: #Mixed
      #lensTransactionPolicyName: #PessimisticRR
      #validity: #installed)

Fig. 12. Methods dataModelSpecForStructureTypeSpecs: and dataModelTemplate (Part 3)

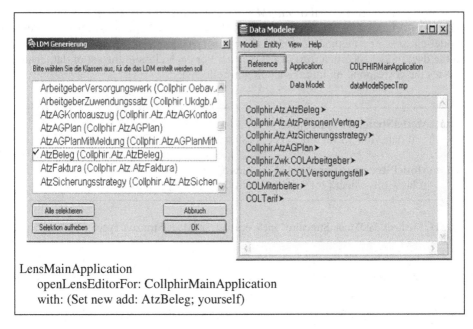

Fig. 13. LensEditor for Class Data Models

4.4 Integration Into the Lens Modeling Tools

Now, the integration into the lens modeling tools is explained. One of our goals was to support the lens modeling tools so that each developer can use these tools in the usual way. Otherwise, the acceptance of the new approach would only be low[8].

The first tool, which we want to support, is the lens editor. The lens editor shows the classes of a data model. Therefore, we provide an opportunity to generate a lens data model for a single class or a set of classes. This is shown in Figure 13. We extend the lens editor by a further selection dialog, which allows the selection of data classes. The method *openLensEditorFor:with:* is called for the set of selected classes. In the example, only class *AtzBeleg* is chosen. The method *openLensEditorFor:with:* calculates all classes, which are needed to construct a complete data model. Therefore, the data model contains not only class *AtzBeleg* but also further classes, which are referred to by *AtzBeleg*. The so generated data model can be manipulated in the same way as the old data models.

Secondly, we support the mapping tool. The mapping tool allows the definition of the mapping between variable and column. In the mapping tool only a single class is considered (Figure 14). Therefore, the mapping tool is the suitable place for creating the class data model. We integrated a new menu item *'Generate Lens Mapping for Class...'*, which opens a multi-selection dialog for the class and its superclasses. The *DataModelDefinitionGenerator* generates the method *primDataModelDefinition* for the selected classes. Remember, the method *primLocalDataModelDefinitionChanges* is not generated.

---

[8] The development of new lens tools was beyond the scope of our solution.

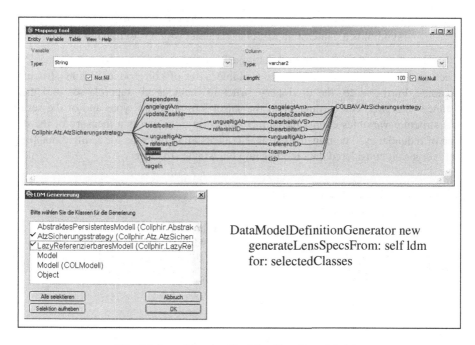

Fig. 14. Lens Mapping Tool for Class Data Models

4.5 DataModelDefinitionGenerator

The class *DataModelDefinitionGenerator* is responsible for the generation of data model fragments. We use the *DataModelDefinitionGenerator* for migration of old monolithic *dataModelSpecs* as well as for generating class data models in the mapping tool.

The major steps of the migration process are described in Figure 15. The *DataModelDefinitionGenerator* can transform a set of data models into a nested dictionary structure. This structure is described by the transformation function *T*. The semantic domains are named after their corresponding classes:

$T: IP(LensDataModel) \rightarrow Dictionary[Class, Dictionary[Symbol, Collection]]$
with:

- $IP(X)$ is the power set of X with: $IP(X) =_{df} \{S: S \subseteq X\}$
- $aDictionary =_{df} \{key_i \rightarrow value_i : i = 1..n\}$
- $T(\{aLensDataModel_i : i = 1.. n\}) =_{df} \{cl \rightarrow aDictionary_{cl} :$

$$\exists k \; \exists s \; (s <_i cl \land$$

$$LensStructureType_s \in aLensDataModel_k \land k \in \{1, ..,n\})^9\}$$

- $aDictionary_{cl} =_{df} \{\#type \rightarrow Set[LensStructureType],$

$$\#variables \rightarrow aDictionary_{cl, variables}\}$$

---

[9] There exists a number *k* and a subclass *s* with the following property: The class *s* is a subclass of *cl* and a *LensStructureType* for class *s* is a member of the *LensDatamodel* with number *k*.

- *aDictionary $_{cl, variables}$* =$_{df}$ *{symbol → Set[LensStructureVariable]:*
    symbol is a name of an instance variable, which is defined in the class *cl}*

For each class the structure of dictionaries collects a set of corresponding lens structure types and for each instance variable a set of corresponding lens structure variables. Furthermore, the dictionary structure includes all superclasses and their instance variables. The cardinality of the set of lens structure types and of the set of lens structure variables counts the number of definitions and is a measure of the degree of redundancy. The transformation T collects all definitions for a single mapping and merges all considered data models into one single structure.

I).   **transformation T**
    generator := DataModelDefinitionGenerator new
        add: AtzMainApplication dataSpec: #dataModelSpec;
        add: ZwkMainApplication dataSpec: #dataModelSpec;
        yourself.

II).   **conflict reports**
    generator report

III).   **data model classes**
    generator
        generateDataModelClassesFor: AtzMainApplication
        dataSpec: #dataModelSpec .

IV).   **generating of all classes**
    generator generate

    generating of a subset of classes
    generator
        generateLensSpecsFrom: ldm
        for: (Set new add: Rente; add: COLAZ03; add: COLAZRR; yourself)

Fig. 15. Migration Process

Figure 16 illustrates the transformation and shows a simplified object view of transformation T^{10}. The dictionaries cluster and order the information hierarchical. The hierarchy-levels are determined by the structure of a lens data model. The essential information is in the leaves of this tree. The class is associated with its lens structure types. Each instance variable is associated with its lens structure variables. These lens structure variables are collected from all subclasses of the class, which occur in the data models.

---

[10] We use a simplified notation that is inspired by the object diagrams of UML ([21]).

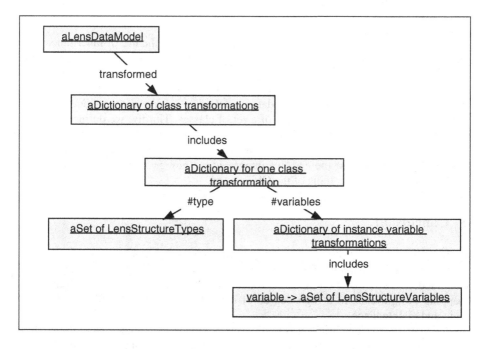

Fig. 16. Simplified Object View of Transformation T

In the following step, we calculated the conflicts between the different definitions of an entity. Here, conflicts during the migration process were handled by a two-step strategy. At first, we eliminated trivial conflict cases and tried to resolve as much conflicts as possible. For example, if different max column constraints occur, then we chose often the weakest one. Then we used pair reviews and decided, which mapping should become the standard. In a second step, we supported different mappings by using the methods *primLocalDataModelDefinitionChanges* and *adaptDataModel*, which allows overriding already generated properties.

After that, we generate the code in two steps. First, we generate the method *dataModelClasses* for the application. Then we generate the *primDataModelDefinition* method from the corresponding *dictionary $_{cl}$*. The method *primDataModelDefinition* is an aggregation of all lens structure variables of the instance variables, which are defined in this class. Therefore, the method includes literal encodings for each self-defined instance variable. Simple data mappings are inlined. Complicated mappings for foreign key relationships are extracted in separate methods.

For the code generation itself we use common Smalltalk techniques. We defined methods for invariant code fragments and methods, which provides a string representation for related parts of the mapping like table name, primary key, or variables. Then we used a stream to merge this fragments. The result is the source string of a Smalltalk method that we compiled in the metaclass of the considered class in the protocol *'lens data model specs'*.

4.6 Summary

The general aspects of our solution are modularization and the use of inheritance. The modularization of the ObjectLens was a four-step process. Firstly, we defined the structure of the specifications of the single data classes. Each data class got a description for its lens structure type. Secondly, we defined the generation of the data model specification of the application. The data model specification of an application is the sum of the data model specifications of a set of classes. Thirdly, we defined a migration process, which translates the old data model specifications into the new structure. The generation process was mostly automatic. Conflict handling was semi-automatic and uses pair reviews. At the end, we integrated the new procedure for defining data models into the modeling tools of the ObjectLens.

5 Conclusion

In this paper, we described an approach to replace the huge monolithic data model specification of the ObjectLens by modular data model specifications and generated data models. In connection with a product line strategy, the old monolithic OR-mapping design leads to a high degree of redundancy, which complicates development and maintenance.

The main idea of our solution is to describe the mappings of each class in the class itself using inheritance and generate the whole specification from a list of single class data models. In this way, declarative and generative programming techniques are combined.

After some months of productive use, we can claim that we achieved our goals. The proposed solution works well. We migrated all old data model specifications of all our applications to the new procedure. The integration of different domain modules is simplified. Often, only the method *dataModelClasses* needs to be adapted. The class data model specifications lead to uniform specifications with lower definition conflicts. The creation and maintenance of the small class data definitions is much easier then the old copy&paste approach. Furthermore, the support of inheritance leads to a 'single point of definition' approach and reduces redundancy extremely. Refactoring or extending class hierarchies is much easier now.

On the implementation stage, we decided to reuse as much as possible from the ObjectLens. Therefore, the data model mappings of the classes use the same lens literal encoding like the original specifications. The class *DataModelDefinitionGenerator*, which we used at first for the migration process, was also suitable for the generation of the *primDataModelDefinition* methods by the mapping tool. The initial *primDataModelDefinition* methods were generated from the old existing *dataModelSpecs*.

On the tools stage, the lens modeling tools were extended to support class data models. The extended lens editor provides support for editing lens data models, which are constructed from a set of classes. The extended mapping tool supports the generation of the method *primDataModelDefinition*, which is the central part of the definition of the lens structure type of a class.

References

[1] Abadi, M.; Cardelli, L.: *"A Theory of Objects"* Springer. New York. 1996.

[2] Alpert, S. R.; Brown, K.; Woolf, B.: *"The Design Patterns Smalltalk Companion"* Addison-Wesley. Reading (Massachusetts). 1998.

[3] Bauer, C.; King, G.: *"Hibernate in Action"* Manning. Greenwich. 2004.

[4] Brown, K.; Whitenack, B.: *"Crossing Chasms for Object-Relational Integration"* in: *"Proceedings of the 3rd Conference on the Pattern Languages of Programs"* 1996.

[5] Cincom Systems: *"VisualWorks: Version 7.2.1, Database Application Developer's Guide"*. Cincom Systems. 2003. www.cincom.com/smalltalk

[6] Cincom Systems: *"VisualWorks: Version 7.2.1, Application Developer's Guide"*. Cincom Systems. 2003. www.cincom.com/smalltalk

[7] Cook, W.; Hill, W.; Canning, P.: *"Inheritance Is Not Subtyping"* in: *"POPL 1990"* pp. 125-135.

[8] Copeland, G.; Maier, D.: *"Making Smalltalk a Database System"* in: *"SIGMOD Record"* Volume 14. Issue 2. 1984. pp. 316-325.

[9] Date, C. J.: *"An Introduction to Database Systems"* Volume 1. Addison-Wesley. Reading (Massachusetts). 6. Edition. 1995.

[10] Elmasari, R.; Navathe, S.: *"Fundamentals of Database Systems"* Cummings Publishing. Redwood City. 1989.

[11] GemsStone Systems: *"GemStone Documentation: Version 5.0"* GemStone Systems, Inc. Juli 1996.

[12] Gamma, E.; Helm, R.; Johnson, R. E.; Vlissides, J.: *"Design Patterns CD: Elements of Reusable Object-Oriented Software"* Addison-Wesley. 1998.

[13] Howard, T.: *"The Smalltalk Developer's Guide to VisualWorks"* SIGS. New York. 1995.

[14] IBL Ingenieurbüro Letters GmbH: *"Polar(R) : Ein Werkzeug zur Abbildung objektorientierter Strukturen auf relationale Datenbanken (Produktpräsentation)"* in: *"Tagungsband STJA '98: Smalltalk und Java in Industrie und Ausbildung"* 1998.

[15] Keller, W.; Coldewey, J.: *"A Design Cookbook for Business Information Systems"* sd&m report. 1996.

[16] Knight, A.: *"Tutorial Using Glorp"* in: *"Proccedings of Smalltalk Solutions' 2004"* 2004. www.glorp.org

[17] Meyer, B.: *"Object-oriented Software Construction"* 2. Edition. Prentice Hall. 1997.

[18] MicroDoc GmbH: *"MicroDoc Persistence Frameworks für Smalltalk und Java: (Produktpräsentation)"* in: *"Tagungsband STJA '98: Smalltalk und Java in Industrie und Ausbildung"* 1998.

[19] ParcPlace Systems: *"VisualWorks: Version 2.0"*. Cincom Systems. 2003.

[20] Prasse, M.: *"Entwicklung und Formalisierung eines objektorientierten Sprachmodells als Grundlage für MEMO-OML"* Fölbach. Koblenz. 2002.

[21] Rumbaugh, J.; Jacobson, I.; Booch, G.: *"The Unified Modeling Language Reference Manual"* Addison-Wesley. 1999.

[22] Roos, R. M.: *"Java Data Objects"* Addison-Wesley. Boston. 2003.

[23] The Object People GmbH: *"TOPLink: Persistenzframework für Smalltalk und Java (Produktpräsentation)"* in: *"Tagungsband STJA '98: Smalltalk und Java in Industrie und Ausbildung"* 1998.

[24] Woolf, B.: *"Understanding and Using ValueModels"* Whitepaper. Knowledge Systems Corporation. 1994.

Meta-driven Browsers*

Alexandre Bergel[1], Stéphane Ducasse[2], Colin Putney[3], and Roel Wuyts[4]

[1] DSG, Trinity College Dublin, Ireland
Alexandre.Bergel@cs.tcd.ie
[2] LISTIC University of Savoie, France & University of Bern, Switzerland
stephane.ducasse@univ-savoie.fr
[3] Wiresong, Canada
cputney@wiresong.ca
[4] Université Libre de Bruxelles, Belgium
Roel.Wuyts@ulb.ac.be

Abstract. Smalltalk is not only an object-oriented programming language; it is also known for its extensive integrated development environment supporting interactive and dynamic programming. While the default tools are adequate for browsing the code and developing applications, it is often cumbersome to extend the environment to support new language constructs or to build additional tools supporting new ways of navigating and presenting source code. In this paper, we present the OmniBrowser, a browser framework that supports the definition of browsers based on an explicit metamodel. With OmniBrowser a domain model is described in a graph and the navigation in this graph is specified in its associated metagraph. We present how new browsers are built from predefined parts and how new tools are easily described. The browser framework is implemented in the Squeak Smalltalk environment. This paper shows several concrete instantiations of the framework: a remake of the ubiquitous Smalltalk System Browser, and a coverage browser.

Keywords: Tools, MetaModeling, UI, Browsers, Squeak.

1 Introduction

Smalltalk is an object-oriented language featuring a complete development environment supporting interactive and dynamic programming [GR83, Gol84]. While the default environment already supports advanced ways of navigating source code and fluid development since the eighties, new browsers have been developed over the years: the *Refactoring Browser* [FBB+99, RBJO96, RBJ97] which was the first system browser supporting refactoring, the *StarBrowser* [WD04]

---

* We gratefully acknowledge the financial support of the Swiss National Science Foundation Recast (SNF 2000-061655.00/1), the Cook ANR french projects and the Science Foundation Ireland and Lero - the Irish Software Engineering Research Centre.

W. De Meuter (Ed.): ISC 2006, LNCS 4406, pp. 134–156, 2007.

which supports smart groups, a browser for incremental development supporting visual feedback of undefined methods [SB04] and the *Whiskers* browser that
shows multiple methods at the same time maximizing the screen space. Strong-
Talk, a more exotic Smalltalk version featuring optional typing, offered a glyph
based browsing environment.

The problem when building all of these browsers is that they are always rebuilt
from scratch because there hardly exists any domain models or frameworks for
building such development tools. In fact, the current browsers in most Smalltalk
environments are hard to extend for two reasons: (a) they are monolythic applications that are not really meant to be included elsewhere, and (b) the navigation
and interaction of the end-user with the browsers is typically hardcoded in the
browser UI elements, and is therefore hard to change or extend.

Note that some Smalltalk environments allow one to embed applications
within each-other. VisualWorks for example has a notion of *subcanvases* which
can be used to that end. This helps to reduce the problem (a) in the previous
paragraph, but not problem (b) of the hardcoding of the the navigation and interaction in the browser UI elements. Other browsers are designed with a certain
amount of customizability in mind, and are therefore easier to extend, but even
those lack explicit descriptions of the navigation.

As was already reported by Steyaert et al. [SLMD96], we conclude that current visual application builders and application frameworks do not live up to
their expectations of rapid application development or non-programming-expert
application development. They fall short when compared to component-oriented
development environments in which applications are built with components that
have a strong affinity with the problem domain (*i.e.*, being domain-specific).

In this paper we present OmniBrowser, a framework to define and compose
new browsers. In OmniBrowser framework, a browser is a graphical list-oriented
tool to navigate and edit an arbitrary domain. The most common representative
of this category of tools is the Smalltalk system browser, which is used to navigate and edit Smalltalk source code. In OmniBrowser framework, a browser is
described by a domain model and a metagraph which specifies how the domain
space is navigated through. Widgets such as list menus and text panels are used
to display information gathered from a particular path in the metagraph. Although widgets are programmatically composed, the OmniBrowser framework
framework supports their interaction.

The contributions of this article are: the description of a metadriven framework to build system browsers and the application of the framework to build
some tools. In Section 2 we describe difficulties and challenges to define states
and flow between those states for a graphical user interface. In Section 3 we
present the key entities of OmniBrowser framework. In Section 4 we present
the OmniBrowser-based system browser and in Section 5 we describe the coverage code browser. In Section 6 we discuss about properties of the OmniBrowser
framework. In Section 7 we provide an overview of related work. In Section 8 we
conclude by summarizing the presented work.

2   Defining and Maintaining the State of a Graphical User Interface

In this section we stress some of the problems encountered when building complex tools such as an advanced code editor.

The state of a graphical user interface (GUI) is defined as a collection of the states of the widgets making up the interface. The state of a widget refers to the state the widget is in. It is modified whenever an end-user performs an action on this widget such as clicking a button or selecting an entry in a menu. Therefore, a GUI has a high number of different states. Asserting the validity for each of these states is crucial to avoid broken or inconsistent interfaces.

Given the potential high number of different states of a GUI, asserting the validity of a GUI is a challenging task. Let's illustrate this situation with the Smalltalk system browser, a graphical tool to edit and navigate into Smalltalk source code.

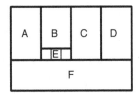

Fig. 1. The traditional Smalltalk System Browser roughly depicted

Figure 1 depicts the different widgets of a traditional Smalltalk class system browser (see Figure 7 for a real picture). Without entering into details, A, B, C and D are lists that show class categories (groups of classes), classes, method protocols (groups of methods) and methods. E is a radio button composed of three choices and F is a text pane.

Pane A lists the categories in the system. Selecting a category in this list, makes the classes in that category appear in pane B. Selecting a class results in the protocols for that class being shown in pane C, and selecting a protocol lists the method names in pane D. Switch E controls whether the class or the metaclass is being edited, and therefore whether the protocols and methods shown are instance level or class level methods. Pane F is a text pane that gives feedback on whatever is selected in the top panes, always displaying the most specific information possible. For example, when a user has selected a method in a protocol in a class in a certain category, pane F shows the definition of that method (and not the definition of the class of that method).

The description of how the browser works shows a number of navigation invariants that need to be kept when implementing the browser. For example, the selections goes from left to right: it is not possible to have methods listed in pane E with pane D being empty.

Invariants such as the one given above need to be implemented and checked when building a browser. So we are dealing with writing an application that deals with a potentially very big number of states in which only certain transitions between states need to be allowed (the ones that correspond to navigations the user of the browser is allowed to do). Whenever a user clicks on widgets that make up the GUI of the browser, the state of one or more widgets is changed, and possibly new navigation possibilities are open up (being able to select a method name, for example) while other ones will no longer be possible (not being able to select a method name when no protocol is selected). To deal with the fact that a widget can be in an inconsistent state, developers often rely on guards: the method performing an action in reaction of an user action always checks whether the state is actually correct or not nil.

In addition the state management is often spread over the UI elements. This leads to code with complex logic (and often bogus). In addition it makes tool elements difficult to extend and reuse in different context.

The problem when building a browser is in representing the mapping from the intended navigation model to the domain model and widgets. Even though graphical framework like MVC [Ree79, Ree] and Coral [SM88] offer ways to modularize the model and the graphical user interface, they do not provide means (i) to preserve consistency of the interface by restricting unexpected state transition to happen and (ii) to keep the widgets synchronized with each other [KP88].

In the next section, we describe a new framework to design browsers where the domain model is distinct from the navigation space. This latter being described by a metagraph. The state of a browser is defined by a path in this metagraph.

3   Defining a Browser: A Graph and a Metagraph

The domain of the OmniBrowser framework is *browsers*, applications with a graphical user interface that are used to navigate a graph of domain elements. When instantiating the OmniBrowser framework to create a browser for a particular domain, the domain elements need to be specified, as well as the desired navigation paths between them.

The OmniBrowser framework is structured around (i) an explicit domain model and (ii) a metagraph, a state machine, that specifies the navigation in and interaction with the domain model. The user interface is constructed by the framework, and uses a layout similar to the Smalltalk System Browser, with two horizontal parts. The top part is a column-based section where the navigation is done. The bottom half is a text pane.

Section 3.1 explains the major classes that make up the OmniBrowser framework. Section 3.2 shows a concrete instantiation to build a file browser. Section 3.3 goes in some more detail and describes the core behavior of the framework. Section 3.4 explains how the widgets are glued together.

3.1   Overview of the OmniBrowser Framework

The major classes that make up the OmniBrowser framework are presented in Figure 2, and explained briefly in the rest of this section.

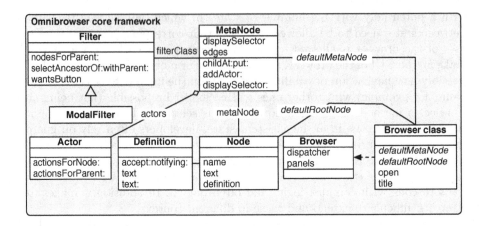

Fig. 2. Core of the OmniBrowser framework

Browser. A *browser* is a graphical tool to navigate and edit a domain space. This domain has to be described in terms of a directed cyclic graph (DCG). It is cyclic because for example file systems or structural meta models of programming language (*i.e.*, packages, classes, methods...) contain cycles, and we need to be able to model those. The domain graph has to have an entry point, its root. The path from this root to a particular node corresponds to a state of the browser is defined by a particular combination of user actions (such as menu selections or button presses). The navigation of this domain graph is specified in a *metagraph*, a state machine describing the states and their possible transitions.

Node. A *node* is a wrapper for a domain object, and has two responsibilities: rendering the domain object, and returning domain nodes. Note that how the domain graph can be navigated is implemented in the *metagraph*.

Metagraph. A browser's *metagraph* defines the way in which the user may traverse the graph of domain objects. A metagraph is composed of metanodes and metaedges. A metanode references a filter (described below) and a set of actors. The metanode does not have the knowledge of the domain nodes, however each node is associated to a metanode. Transitions between metanodes are defined by metaedges. When a metaedge is traversed (*i.e.*, result of pressing a button or selecting an entry list), siblings nodes are created from a given node by invoking a method that has the name of the metaedge.

Actor. An *actor* is a basic unit of domain-related functionality. Actors are attached to metanodes, and supply the *actions* used to interact with objects wrapped by nodes. For instance, *actors* are used to build context menus and buttons in the *browser*.

Action. An *Action* represents a Command [ABW98] for manipulating, interacting and navigating with the graph domain. Actions can be made available through menus or buttons in the browser. They carry information on how they should be presented to the user and are responsible for handling exceptions that can occur when they are triggered. Actions are created by actors.

Filter. The metagraph describes a state machine. When the browser is in a state where there are two transitions available. The user is the one that decides which transition to follow. To allow that to happen OmniBrowser framework displays the possibilities to the user. From all the possible transitions, OmniBrowser framework fetches all the nodes that represent the states the user could arrive at by following those transitions and list them in the next column. Note that the transition is not actually make yet, and the definition pane is still displaying the class definition. Once a click is made, the transition actually happens, the pane definition is updated (and perhaps other panes such as button bars) and it gathers the next round of possible transitions.

A filter provides a strategy for filtering out some of the nodes from the display. If a node is the starting point of several edges, a filter is needed to filter out all but one edges to determine which path has to be taken in the metagraph.

Definition. While navigating in the domain space, information about the selected node is displayed in a dedicated textual panel. If edition is expected by the browser user, then a definition is necessary to handle commitment (*i.e.*, an *accept* in the Smalltalk terminology). A definition is produced by a node.

3.2   A Simple Example: A File Browser

To illustrate how the OmniBrowser framework is instantiated, we describe the implementation of a simple file browser supporting the navigation in directories and files [Hal05].

Figure 3 shows the file browser in action. A browser is opened by evaluating FileBrowser open in a workspace. The navigation columns in the case of a file browser are used to navigate through directories, where every column lists the contents of the directory selected in its left column, similar to the *Column View* of the Finder in the Mac OS-X operating system. Note that we can have an infinite numbers of pane navigating through the file system. The horizontal scrollbar lets the user browse the directory structure. A text panel below the columns displays additional properties of the currently selected directory or file and provides means to manipulate these properties.

Node definitions. Nodes wrap objects of the browsed domain. First the class FileNode a subclass of Node is created which represents a file. A file node is identified by a full path name, stored in a variable. The name of the node is simply the name of the file selected:

FileNode≫name
     ^ (FileDirectory directoryEntryFor: path) name.

A text containing information about the selected file is returned by the method text:

FileNode≫text
   ^ 'First 1000 characters: ', String cr,
     ((FileStream readOnlyFileNamed: path) converter: Latin1TextConverter new;
        next: 1000) asString

A directory node is a kind of file that contains directories and files. The methods files and directories are defined on the class DirectoryNode.

DirectoryNode≫directories
   | dir |
   dir := FileDirectory on: path.
   ^ dir directoryNames collect: [:each |
                DirectoryNode new path: (dir fullNameFor: each)]

DirectoryNode≫files
   | dir |
   dir := FileDirectory on: path.
   ^ dir fileNames collect: [:each |
     FileNode new path: (dir fullNameFor: each)]

The implementation shows the two responsibilities of a node: rendering itself (implemented in the text method), and calculating the nodes reachable from a node (in the directories and files methods).

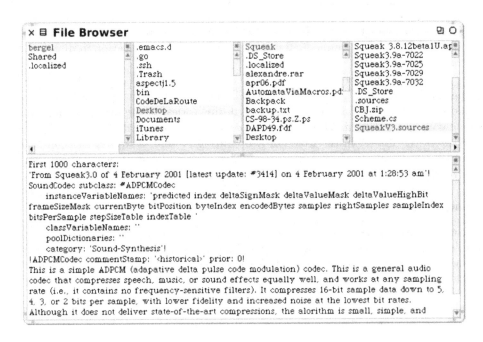

Fig. 3. A minimal file browser based on OmniBrowser

Action Definitions. The user can perform some actions on selected files. Those are implemented in the class FileActor which inherits from Actor. Action are commands with user-interface information such as icon.

```
FileActor≫actionsForNode: aNode
    ^ {OBAction
            label: 'remove'
            receiver: self
            selector: #removeFile:
            arguments: {aNode}
            keystroke: $x
            icon: MenuIcons smallCancelIcon.
        OBAction
            label: 'rename'
            receiver: self
            selector: #renameFile:
            arguments: {aNode}}


FileActor≫removeFile: aNode
    "Remove the file designed by aNode"
    ...


FileActor≫renameFile: aNode
    "Rename the file designed by aNode"
    ...
```

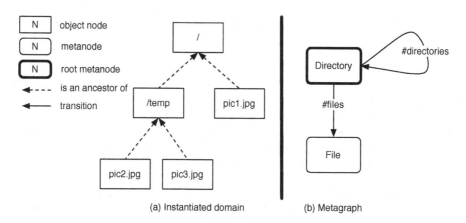

(a) Instantiated domain   (b) Metagraph

Fig. 4. A filesystem (as a graph) (a) and its corresponding metagraph (b)

Metagraph Definition. Figure 4 shows a metagraph describing a filesystem. Two metanodes, Directory and File, compose this metagraph. The navigation between these nodes is defined by two transitions, files and directories. The starting point in a metagraph is designated by a root metanode.

The metagraph is implemented in the class FileBrowser. The methods default-MetaNode and defaultRootNode are defined on the class side of FileBrowser. These methods define the metagraph and gives the root node, respectively:

FileBrowser class≫defaultMetaNode
    "returns the directory metanode that acts as the root metanode"

```
| directory file |
directory := OBMetaNode named: 'Directory'.

file := OBMetaNode named: 'File'.
file addActor: FileActor new.

directory
    childAt: #directories put: directory;
    childAt: #files put: file;
    addActor: FileActor new.

^ directory
```

FileBrowser class≫defaultRootNode
    ^ DirectoryNode new path: '/'

When one of the two #directories and #files metaedges is traversed, the name of this metaedge is used as a message name sent to the metanode's node.

3.3   Core Behavior of the Framework

The core of the OmniBrowser framework is composed of 8 classes (Figure 2). We denote the Smalltalk metaclass hierarchy by a dashed arrow.

The metaclass of the class Browser is Browser class. It defines two abstract methods defaultMetaNode and defaultRootNode. These methods are abstract, they therefore need to be overridden in subclasses. These methods are called when a browser is instantiated. The methods defaultMetaNode and default-RootNode returns the root metanode and the root domain node, respectively. A browser is opened by sending the message open to an instance of the class Browser.

The navigation graph is built with instances of the class MetaNode. Transitions are built by sending messages childAt: selector put: metanode to a MetaNode instance. These has the effect to create a metaedge named selector leading away the metanode receiver of the message and metanode.

At runtime, the graph traversal is triggered by user actions (*e.g.*, pressing a button or selecting a list entry) which sends the metaedge's name to the node that is currently selected. Actors are attached to a metanode using the method addActor:. The rendering of a node is performed by invoking on the domain node the selector stored in the variable displaySelector in the metanode.

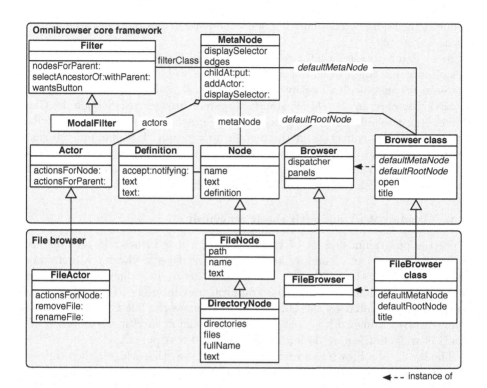

Fig. 5. Core of the OmniBrowser framework and its extension for the file browser

The class Actor is normally instantiated by metanodes and is used to define node related actions. The method actionsForNode: may be overridden in subclasses to answer an ordered collection of actions. The method actionsForParent: is used to specify actions that are independent from any nodes. These actions are typically shown on a menu when no node is selected.

The class Node represents an element of the domain graph. Each node has a name. This name is used when lists of nodes are displayed in the navigation columns of the browser. When a node is selected in a list, information related to this node needs to be displayed in the bottom text pane. When the node is not supposed to be edited, the message text is sent to it, returning a string displayed in the bottom pane. When it is editable, it is sent the message definition which needs to return an instance of a subclass of Definition. Note that the nodes do not need to be configured to be editable or not. When they implement a method definition, this will be used and the node will be editable. If that method is not present, then the method text is used.

When the browser is in a state where several transitions are available, it displays the possibilities to the user. From all the possible transitions, OmniBrowser framework fetches all the nodes that represent the states the user could arrive at by following those transitions and list them in the next column. Once a selection is made, the transition actually happens, the pane definition is updated and the process repeats.

As explained before, a filter or modal filter can be used to select only a number of outgoing edges when not all of them need to be shown to the user. This is useful for instance to display the instance side, comments, or class side of a particular class in the classic standard system browser (cf. Section 4). Class Filter is responsible for filtering nodes in the graph. The method nodesForParent: computes a transition in the domain metagraph. This method returns a list of nodes obtained from a given node passed as argument. The class Filter is subclassed into ModalFilter, a handy filter that represents transitions in the metagraph that can be traversed by using a radio button in the GUI.

3.4   Glueing Widgets with the Metagraph

From the programmer point of view, creating a new browser implies defining a domain model (set of nodes like FileNode and DirectoryNode), a metagraph intended to steer the navigation and a set of actors to define interaction and actions with domain elements. The graphical user interface of a browser is automatically generated by the OmniBrowser framework. The GUI generated by OmniBrowser framework is contained in one window, and it is composed of 4 kinds of widgets (lists, radio buttons, menus and text panes).

The layout of a browser can be redefined and use other widgets then the ones described above, but those are then not used by the metagraph. For instance, the OmniBrowser framework-based system browser uses a toolbar widget that allows a user to launch other kind of browsers like the variable and hierarchy browsers. We will not describe how to use other widgets, as this is outside the scope of this paper.

Lists. Navigation in OmniBrowser framework is rendered with a set of lists and triggered by selecting one entry in a list. Lists displayed in a browser are ordered and are displayed from left to right. Traversing a new metanode, by selecting a node in a list A, triggers the construction of a set of nodes intended to fill a list B. List B follows list A.

The root of a metagraph corresponds to the left-most list. The number of lists displayed is equal to the depth of the metagraph. The depth of the system browser metagraph (Figure 9) is 4, therefore the system browser has 4 panes (Figure 7). Because the metagraph of a filesystem may contain cycles (*i.e.*, a directory may contain directories, as shown in Figure 4), the number of lists in the browser increases for each directory selected in the right-most list. Therefore a horizontal scrollbar is used to keep the width of the browser constant, yet displaying a potentially infinite number of lists in the top half.

Radio buttons. A modal filter in the metagraph is represented in the GUI by a radio button. Each edge leading away from the filter is represented as a button in the radio button. Only one button can be selected at a time in the radio button, and the associated choice is used to determine the outgoing edges. For example, the second list in the system browser contains the three buttons instance, ? and class as shown the transition from the environment to the three metanodes class, class comment and metaclass in Figure 7.

Menus. A menu can be displayed for each list widget of a browser. Typically such a menu displays a list of actions that can be executed by a browser user. These actions enable interaction with the domain model, however they do not allow further navigation in the metagraph.

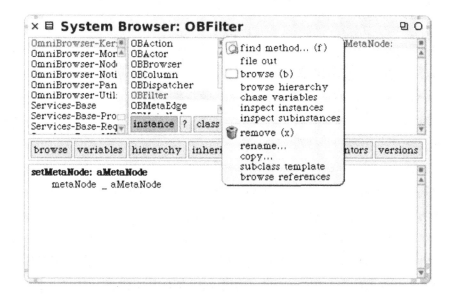

Fig. 6. Example of menu in the OmniBrowser framework system browser

Figure 6 shows an example of a menu offering actions related to a class. These correspond to the list of actions returned by the method actionsForNode: in the class ClassActor.

Text pane. When a node is selected in a list, some information related to this node is displayed in a text pane. Committing a change in the text pane sends the message accept: newText notifying: aController to the definition shown in this pane. A browser contains only one text pane.

4   The OmniBrowser-Based System Browser

In this section we show how the framework is used to implement the traditional class system browser.

4.1   The Smalltalk System Browser

The system browser is probably the most important tool offered by the Smalltalk programming environment. It enables code navigation and code editing. Figure 7

146   A. Bergel et al.

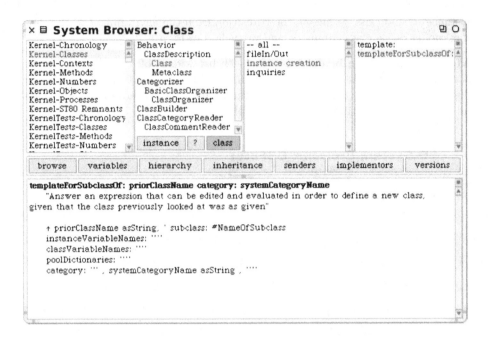

Fig. 7. OmniBrowser framework based Smalltalk system browser

shows the graphical user interface of this browser, and how it appears to the Smalltalk programmer.

This browser just replicates the traditional four panes system browser discussed in Section 2. The system browser is mainly composed of four lists (upper part) and a panel (lower part). From left to right, the lists represent (i) class categories, (ii) classes contained in the selected class category, (iii) method categories defined in the selected class to which the − all − category is added, and (iv) the list of methods defined in the selected method category. On Figure 7, the class named Class, which belongs to the class category Kernel-Classes is selected. Class has three methods categories, plus the − all − one. The method template-ForSubclassOf:category contained in the instance creation method category is selected.

The lower part of the system browser contains a large textual panel display information about the current selection in the lists. Selecting a class category makes the render display a class template intended to be filled out to create a new class in the system. If a class is selected, then this panel shows the definition of this class. If a method is selected, then the definition of this method is displayed. The text contained in the panel can be edited. The effect of this is to create a new class, a new methods, or changing the definition of a class (*e.g.*, adding a new variable, changing the superclass) or redefining a method.

In the upper part, the class list contains three buttons (titled instance, ? and class) to let one switch between different "views" on a class: the class definition, its comment and the definition of its metaclass. Just above the panel, there is a toolbar intended to open more specific browsers like a hierarchy browser and a variable access browser.

4.2   System Browser Internals

The Omnibrowser-based implementation of the Squeak system browser is composed of 19 classes (2 actors, 2 classes for the browser, 3 classes for the definitions of classes, methods and organization, 10 classes defining nodes and 2 utility classes with abstractions to help link the browser and the system). 220 methods are spread over these 19 classes. Figure 8 shows the classes in OmniBrowser framework that need to be subclassed to produce the system browser. Note that the two utility classes are not represented on the picture.

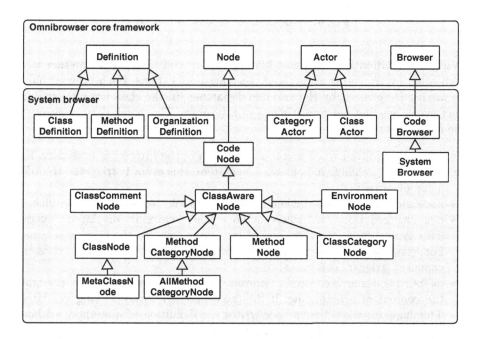

Fig. 8. Extension of OmniBrowser framework to define the system browser

Compared to the default implementation of the Squeak System Browser this is less code and better factored. In addition other code-browsers can freely reuse these parts.

Figure 9 depicts the metagraph of the system browser. The metanode environment contains information about class categories. The filter is used to select what has to be displayed from the selected class (*i.e.*, the class definition, its comment or the metaclass definition). A class and a metaclass have a list of method categories, including the − all − method category that shows a list of methods.

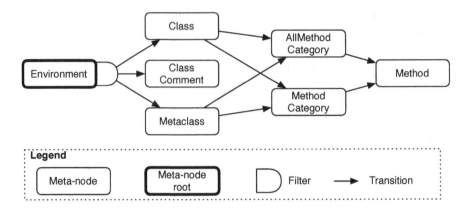

Fig. 9. Metagraph of the system browser

Widgets notification. Widgets like menu lists and text panels interact with each other by triggering events and receiving notifications. Each browser has a dispatcher (referenced by the variable dispatcher in the class Browser) to conduct events passing between widgets of a browser. The vocabulary of events is the following one:

- refresh is emitted when a complete refresh of the browser is necessary. For instance, if a change happens in the system, this event is triggered to order a complete redraw.
- nodeSelected: is emitted when a list entry is selected with a mouse click.
- nodeChanged is emitted when the node that is currently displayed changes. This typically occurs when one of buttons related to the class is selected. For example, if a class is displayed, pressing the button instance, class or comment triggers this event.
- okToChangeNode is emitted to prevent loose some text edition why changing the content of a text panel if this was modified without being validated. This happens when first a user writes the definition of a method, without accepting (*i.e.*, compiling) it, and then another method is selected.

Each graphical widget composing a browser are listeners and can emit events. Creation and registration of widgets as listeners and event emitters is completely transparent to the end user.

State of the browser. Contrary to the original Squeak system browser where each widget state is contained in a dedicated variable, the state of a OmniBrowser framework-based browser is defined as a path in the metagraph starting from the root metanode. Each metanode taking part of this path is associated to a domain node. This preserves the synchronization between different graphical widgets of a browser.

5   The Coverage Browser

The coverage browser is an extension to the system browser to show the coverage of code by unit tests. It extends the system browser in two ways. First of all it appends the percentage of elements covered by tests to the elements in the lists

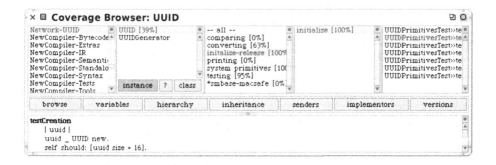

Fig. 10. Screenshot of the coverage browser

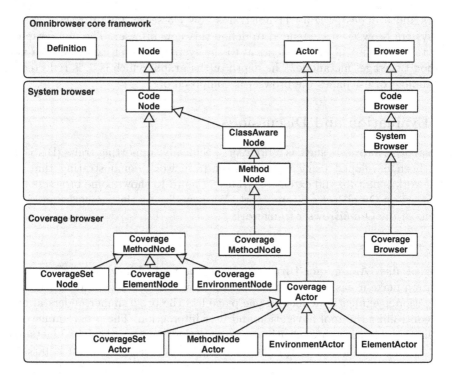

Fig. 11. Extension of Omnibrowser and system browser to define the coverage browser

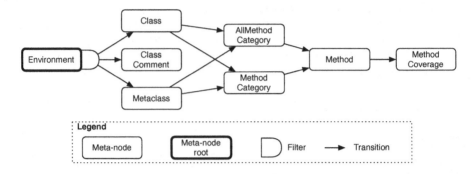

Fig. 12. Metagraph for the coverage browser

making up the browser. Secondly it adds a fifth pane that lists the unit tests that test a selected method. A screenshot is shown in Figure 10. It shows us that 39% of the class UUID is covered by tests, and that the method initialize is covered at 100% by the tests shows in the right-most pane. One of these test is testCreation.

The coverage browser is composed of 11 classes (1 class for the browser, 5 actors and 5 nodes). Figure 11 illustrates how classes in OmniBrowser and in the system browser are extended to define this new browser. The metagraph is depicted in Figure 12 and is identical to the system browser except with a new Method Coverage metanode. The depth of the graph, which is 5, is reflected in the number of list panes the browser is composed of.

6   Evaluation and Discussions

Several other browsers such as a browser specifically supporting traits [DNS+06] have been developed using OmniBrowser framework demonstrating that the framework is mature and extensible [RJ97]. Figure 13 shows some browsers that are based on OmniBrowser framework. We now discuss the strengths and limitations of the OmniBrowser framework.

6.1   Strengths

Ease of use. As any good framework, extending it following the framework intention make it easy to specify advanced browsers. The fact that the browser navigation is explicitly defined in one place lets the programmer understanding and controlling the tool navigation and user interaction. The programmer does not have the burden to explicitly create and glue together the UI widgets and their specific layout. Extra decorating widgets such as extra-menu is possible and defined independently. Still the programmer focuses on the key domain of the browser: its navigation and the interaction with the user.

Explicit state transitions. Maintaining coherence among different widgets and keeping them synchronized is a non-trival issue that, while well supported

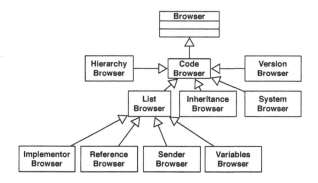

Fig. 13. Some code browsers developed using OmniBrowser framework

by GUI frameworks, is often not well used. For instance, in the original Squeak browser, methods are scattered with checks for nil or 0 values. For instance, the method classComment: aText notifying: aPluggableTextMorph, which is called by the text pane (F widget) to assign a new comment to the selected class (B widget), is:

```
Browser≫classComment: aText notifying: aPluggableTextMorph
    theClass := self selectedClassOrMetaClass.
    theClass
        ifNotNil: [ ... ]
```

The code above copes with the fact that when pressing on the class comment button, there is no warranty that a class is selected. In a good UI design, the comment class button should have been disabled however there is still checks done whether a class is selected or not. Among the 438 accessible methods in the non Omnibrowser-based Squeak class Browser, 63 of them invoke ifNil: to test if a list is selected or not and 62 of them invoke ifNotNil:. Those are not isolated Smalltalk examples. The code that describes some GUI present in the JHotDraw [JHo] contains the pattern checking for a nil value of variables that may reference graphical widgets.

Such as situation does not happen in OmniBrowser framework, as metagraphs are declaratively defined and each metaedge describes an action the user can perform on a browser, states a browser can be in are explicit and fully described.

Separation of domain and navigation. The domain model and its navigation are fully separated: a metanode does not and cannot have a reference to the domain node currently selected and displayed. Therefore both can be reused independently.

6.2   Limitations

Hardcoded flow. As any framework, OmniBrowser framework constraints the space of its own extension. OmniBrowser framework does not support well the definition of navigation not following the left to right list construction (the result of the selection creates a new pane to the right of the current one and the text pane is displayed). For example, building a browser such as Whiskers that displays multiple methods at the same time would require to deeply change the text pane state to keep the status of the currently edited methods.

Currently selected item. The OmniBrowser framework does not easily support the building of advanced browsing facilities such as the one of the Visual-Works standard browser. In VisualWorks, it is possible to select a package, then select one class of this package and as third step see the inheritance hierarchy of this class within the context of the previously selected package. The problem is that conceptually the selected item is not part of the state representation. It is possible using UI events passing among the widgets to implement

7   Related Work

MVC. The Model-View-Controller [KP88, Ree, Ree79] promotes a distinction between three important roles (namely data, output and interaction) that should be reflected in the design of a user interface framework. Those roles were reflected in three abstract superclasses: Model, View, Controller. Still for system browsers, developers consider the model as the entities of the domain and do not have explicit or meta entities describing the navigation within the domain model. Note also that a controller in MVC captures the interaction of users with a widget,and passes this information to the model. The level of abstraction, however, is lower than what is offered by the *Actor* in the OmniBrowser framework, which is not programmed in terms of a widget but in terms of the domain entities.

HotDraw. The state transitions between the possible tools in HotDraw [Joh92] are driven by an explicit state machine and follow an explicit transition structure. There is a graphical editor (constructed with HotDraw itself) to construct the view and edit the state machine. The goal of the state machine is similar to the goal of the metagraph in the OmniBrowser framework: to make navigation explicit. In HotDraw, however, the events to go from one state to another are taken from a limited set of possible actions such as mouse over.

HyperCard. Conceptually, a HyperCard [Goo98] application is a stack of cards. Each card contains some information and links to other cards in the same or other stacks. The information on the cards is shown using text and graphics. The links to other cards are presented as buttons, typically completed with an icon representing the destination card. A user of HyperCard browses the cards of a stack using the link button. Only one card of a stack is displayed at a time. Clicking a link button results in the display of the destination card. When a stack has not only information to be displayed, but also has to exhibit an active behavior, the stack designer has to develop cards by means of a scripting level, on which programming in the dedicated language HyperTalk is supported. Still there is not as such a metagraph describing the navigation of a domain graph.

ApplFLab. Steyaert *et al.* defined the notion of reflective application builder [SHDB96] with as explicit goal to be able to construct and reuse (parametrizable) user interface components. ApplFLab was used to construct several domain specific user interfaces, including browsers in development environments [Wuy96].

ApplFLab structures a software program using four distinct kinds of components:

- a *user interface component* controls the display and the user interaction of a particular piece of information, supplied by the domain model. Note that this component is parametrized by the domain model, and therefore can be reused across different domains.
- an *application model* manages the global behavior of group of interface components. It is responsible for the user interface logic and controls user interface. A same application model can be reused on different domain models and a domain model can have several application models in parallel.
- a *domain model* models the overall functionality of the problem domain and maintains user interface independent constraints.
- a set of *aspects* is needed to separate the domain model from the user interface component.

Interaction between these four components is based on emitting events and being notified. There are three kinds of event: *display*, *notify* and *control*.

The advantage of ApplFLab lies in its notion of parametrized user interface component. A user interface component consists of a GUI description, and parameters to link the component to the domain or to specify other information when it is used in an application. The components are plugged together to form applications. One could for example build a list component, and parametrize it with categories, classes, protocols and selectors to get the four top elements that make a System Browser (as shown in Section 4.1). Combine it with a Text component and the System Browser is complete.

While both ApplFLab and the OmniBrowser make it easy to build browsers, there are some differences. The OmniBrowser is a domain specific approach for building browsers, while ApplFLab is general. So when using ApplFLab to build browser, browser specific components need to be built first, for example to get the left-to-right selection behavior that is built-in with OmniBrowser. ApplFLab also had a steeper learning curve, since building a good reusable component (be it a visual one or a regular one) remains fairly difficult. On the other hand, OmniBrowser offers more built-in behavior which makes it easier to use but also forces certain behavior that might not always be wanted.

ThingLab. Freeman-Benson and Maloney [FB89] wrote ThingLab II, an object-oriented constraint system for direct manipulation user interface implemented in Smalltalk-80. In ThingLab II, user-manipulable entities are collections of objects know as *Things*. ThingLab II provides a large number of primitive Things equivalent to the operations and data structures provided in any high-level language: numerical operations, points, strings, bitmaps, conversion, etc.

A thing is constructed from things objects and constraint objects. Higher-level things can be built out of the lower-level ones. Constraints are either satisfied or they are not satisfied, and they are simple declarative declarations that do not hold state. Browser navigation can be expressed by constraints between the different elements that composed a browser. But there is no explicit distinction between the domain and its navigation.

8   Conclusion

Smalltalk is known for its advanced development environment, featuring advanced browsers that let developers navigate and change code relatively easily.

Building browsers, however, is a daunting task. The main problem is that every navigation action performed by a user in a widget changes the state of that (and possibly other) widgets. Given the high number of possible navigation actions, the complexity of managing the navigation by managing the states of the browser is a very complex task. This can be seen in most current browser implementations, which are complex and hard to extend because the navigation is implicitly encoded in the management of the state of the widgets.

To make it easier to build and extend browsers, this paper introduces a framework for building browsers that is based on modeling user navigation through an explicit graph. In this framework, browsers are built by modeling the domain with *nodes*, expressing the navigation with a *metagraph* and describing the interaction between the browser and the domain through *actors*. The framework uses these descriptions to construct a graphical application. The top half of the application uses lists that allow the user to navigate the described domain. The bottom half of the pane allows to visualize and edit nodes selected in the top half.

The framework is implemented in Squeak Smalltalk through the OmniBrowser framework. The paper showed three concrete instantiations of the framework: a file browser to navigate a file system,a reimplementation of the ubiquitous Smalltalk System Browser, and a code coverage browser. There are more instantiations of the browser that we have not discussed in this paper but that are available. The validation shows that the goals of the frameworks are met. Building the System Browser with the OmniBrowser framework shows that the code is lots simpler. The Code Coverage browser shows that it is easy to extend an existing browser.

For future work we plan to enhance the OmniBrowser framework with the ability to have multiple text panes to be part of a browser. We also plan to extend the framework to support more and richer widgets (such as toolbars and flaps). Last but not least we want to investigate how we can extend the metagraph to look at other ways of navigating it.

Acknowledgment. We would like to thank Niklaus Haldimann and Stefan Reichnart for their use of the OmniBrowser framework.

We gratefully acknowledge the financial support of the french ANR project "Cook: Réarchitecturisation des applications industrielles objets" (JC05 42872) and of the Science Foundation Ireland and Lero — the Irish Software Engineering Research Centre.

References

[ABW98]   Sherman R. Alpert, Kyle Brown, and Bobby Woolf. *The Design Patterns Smalltalk Companion.* Addison Wesley, 1998.

[DNS⁺06]   Stéphane Ducasse, Oscar Nierstrasz, Nathanael Schärli, Roel Wuyts, and Andrew Black. Traits: A mechanism for fine-grained reuse. *ACM Transactions on Programming Languages and Systems*, 28(2):331–388, March 2006.

[FB89]   Bjorn N. Freeman-Benson. A module mechanism for constraints in Smalltalk. In *Proceedings OOPSLA '89, ACM SIGPLAN Notices*, volume 24, pages 389–396, October 1989.

[FBB⁺99]   Martin Fowler, Kent Beck, John Brant, William Opdyke, and Don Roberts. *Refactoring: Improving the Design of Existing Code.* Addison Wesley, 1999.

[Gol84]   Adele Goldberg. *Smalltalk 80: the Interactive Programming Environment.* Addison Wesley, Reading, Mass., 1984.

[Goo98]   Danny Goodman. *The Complete HyperCard 2.2 Handbook.* iUniverse, 1998.

[GR83]   Adele Goldberg and David Robson. *Smalltalk 80: the Language and its Implementation.* Addison Wesley, Reading, Mass., May 1983.

[Hal05]   Niklaus Haldimann. A sophisticated programming environment to cope with scoped changes. Informatikprojekt, University of Bern, December 2005.

[JHo]   Jhotdraw: a java gui framework for technical and structured graphics. http://www.jhotdraw.org.

[Joh92]   Ralph E. Johnson. Documenting frameworks using patterns. In *Proceedings OOPSLA '92*, volume 27, pages 63–76, October 1992.

[KP88]   G. E. Krasner and S. T. Pope. A cookbook for using the model-view-controller user interface paradigm in Smalltalk-80. *Journal of Object-Oriented Programming*, 1(3):26–49, August 1988.

[RBJ97]   Don Roberts, John Brant, and Ralph E. Johnson. A refactoring tool for Smalltalk. *Theory and Practice of Object Systems (TAPOS)*, 3(4):253–263, 1997.

[RBJO96]   Don Roberts, John Brant, Ralph E. Johnson, and Bill Opdyke. An automated refactoring tool. In *Proceedings of ICAST '96, Chicago, IL*, April 1996.

[Ree]   Trygve M. H. Reenskaug. The model-view-controller (mvc) – its past and present. JavaZONE, Oslo, 2003.

[Ree79]   Trygve M. H. Reenskaug. Models - views - controllers, December 1979. http://heim.ifi.uio.no/~trygver/1979/mvc-2/1979-12-MVC.pdf.

[RJ97]   Don Roberts and Ralph E. Johnson. Evolving frameworks: A pattern language for developing object-oriented frameworks. In *Pattern Languages of Program Design 3*. Addison Wesley, 1997.

[SB04]   Nathanael Schärli and Andrew P. Black. A browser for incremental programming. *Computer Languages, Systems and Structures*, 30:79–95, 2004.

[SHDB96]   Patrick Steyaert, Koen De Hondt, Serge Demeyer, and Niels Boyen. Reflective user interface builders. In Chris Zimmerman, editor, *Advances in Object-Oriented Metalevel Architectures and Reflection*, pages 291–309. CRC Press — Boca Raton — Florida, 1996.

[SLMD96]   Patrick Steyaert, Carine Lucas, Kim Mens, and Theo D'Hondt. Reuse Contracts: Managing the Evolution of Reusable Assets. In *Proceedings of OOPSLA '96 (International Conference on Object-Oriented Programming, Systems, Languages, and Applications)*, pages 268–285. ACM Press, 1996.

[SM88]   Pedro Szekely and Brad Myers. A user interface toolkit based on graphical objects and constraints. In *Proceedings OOPSLA '88, ACM SIGPLAN Notices*, volume 23, pages 36–45, November 1988.

[WD04]   Roel Wuyts and Stéphane Ducasse. Unanticipated integration of development tools using the classification model. *Journal of Computer Languages, Systems and Structures*, 30(1-2):63–77, 2004.

[Wuy96]   Roel Wuyts. Class-management using logical queries, application of a reflective user interface builder. In I. Polak, editor, *Proceedings of GRONICS '96*, pages 61–67, 1996.

Author Index

Bergel, Alexandre 66, 134
Brichau, Johan 1

Cañibano, Nicolás 23

D'Hondt, Theo 1
Denker, Marcus 47
Dony, Christophe 91
Ducasse, Stéphane 66, 134

Fabresse, Luc 91
Fortier, Andrés 23

Gordillo, Silvia 23
Grigera, Julián 23
Gybels, Kris 1

Hirschfeld, Robert 1
Huchard, Marianne 91

Kellens, Andy 1

Mens, Kim 1

Nierstrasz, Oscar 66

Prasse, Michael 111
Putney, Colin 134

Rossi, Gustavo 23
Röthlisberger, David 47

Tanter, Éric 47

Wuyts, Roel 66, 134

Vol. 4395: M. Daydé, J.M.L.M. Palma, Á.L.G.A. Coutinho, E. Pacitti, J.C. Lopes (Eds.), High Performance Computing for Computational Science - VEC-PAR 2006. XXIV, 721 pages. 2007.

Vol. 4394: A. Gelbukh (Ed.), Computational Linguistics and Intelligent Text Processing. XVI, 648 pages. 2007.

Vol. 4393: W. Thomas, P. Weil (Eds.), STACS 2007. XVIII, 708 pages. 2007.

Vol. 4392: S.P. Vadhan (Ed.), Theory of Cryptography. XI, 595 pages. 2007.

Vol. 4391: Y. Stylianou, M. Faundez-Zanuy, A. Esposito (Eds.), Progress in Nonlinear Speech Processing. XII, 269 pages. 2007.

Vol. 4390: S.O. Kuznetsov, S. Schmidt (Eds.), Formal Concept Analysis. X, 329 pages. 2007. (Sublibrary LNAI).

Vol. 4389: D. Weyns, H.V.D. Parunak, F. Michel (Eds.), Environments for Multi-Agent Systems III. X, 273 pages. 2007. (Sublibrary LNAI).

Vol. 4385: K. Coninx, K. Luyten, K.A. Schneider (Eds.), Task Models and Diagrams for Users Interface Design. XI, 355 pages. 2007.

Vol. 4384: T. Washio, K. Satoh, H. Takeda, A. Inokuchi (Eds.), New Frontiers in Artificial Intelligence. IX, 401 pages. 2007. (Sublibrary LNAI).

Vol. 4383: E. Bin, A. Ziv, S. Ur (Eds.), Hardware and Software, Verification and Testing. XII, 235 pages. 2007.

Vol. 4381: J. Akiyama, W.Y.C. Chen, M. Kano, X. Li, Q. Yu (Eds.), Discrete Geometry, Combinatorics and Graph Theory. XI, 289 pages. 2007.

Vol. 4380: S. Spaccapietra, P. Atzeni, F. Fages, M.-S. Hacid, M. Kifer, J. Mylopoulos, B. Pernici, P. Shvaiko, J. Trujillo, I. Zaihrayeu (Eds.), Journal on Data Semantics VIII. XV, 219 pages. 2007.

Vol. 4378: I. Virbitskaite, A. Voronkov (Eds.), Perspectives of Systems Informatics. XIV, 496 pages. 2007.

Vol. 4377: M. Abe (Ed.), Topics in Cryptology – CT-RSA 2007. XI, 403 pages. 2006.

Vol. 4376: E. Frachtenberg, U. Schwiegelshohn (Eds.), Job Scheduling Strategies for Parallel Processing. VII, 257 pages. 2007.

Vol. 4374: J.F. Peters, A. Skowron, I. Düntsch, J. Grzymała-Busse, E. Orłowska, L. Polkowski (Eds.), Transactions on Rough Sets VI, Part I. XII, 499 pages. 2007.

Vol. 4373: K. Langendoen, T. Voigt (Eds.), Wireless Sensor Networks. XIII, 358 pages. 2007.

Vol. 4372: M. Kaufmann, D. Wagner (Eds.), Graph Drawing. XIV, 454 pages. 2007.

Vol. 4371: K. Inoue, K. Satoh, F. Toni (Eds.), Computational Logic in Multi-Agent Systems. X, 315 pages. 2007. (Sublibrary LNAI).

Vol. 4370: P.P Lévy, B. Le Grand, F. Poulet, M. Soto, L. Darago, L. Toubiana, J.-F. Vibert (Eds.), Pixelization Paradigm. XV, 279 pages. 2007.

Vol. 4369: M. Umeda, A. Wolf, O. Bartenstein, U. Geske, D. Seipel, O. Takata (Eds.), Declarative Programming for Knowledge Management. X, 229 pages. 2006. (Sublibrary LNAI).

Vol. 4368: T. Erlebach, C. Kaklamanis (Eds.), Approximation and Online Algorithms. X, 345 pages. 2007.

Vol. 4367: K. De Bosschere, D. Kaeli, P. Stenström, D. Whalley, T. Ungerer (Eds.), High Performance Embedded Architectures and Compilers. XI, 307 pages. 2007.

Vol. 4366: K. Tuyls, R. Westra, Y. Saeys, A. Nowé (Eds.), Knowledge Discovery and Emergent Complexity in Bioinformatics. IX, 183 pages. 2007. (Sublibrary LNBI).

Vol. 4364: T. Kühne (Ed.), Models in Software Engineering. XI, 332 pages. 2007.

Vol. 4362: J. van Leeuwen, G.F. Italiano, W. van der Hoek, C. Meinel, H. Sack, F. Plášil (Eds.), SOFSEM 2007: Theory and Practice of Computer Science. XXI, 937 pages. 2007.

Vol. 4361: H.J. Hoogeboom, G. Păun, G. Rozenberg, A. Salomaa (Eds.), Membrane Computing. IX, 555 pages. 2006.

Vol. 4360: W. Dubitzky, A. Schuster, P.M.A. Sloot, M. Schroeder, M. Romberg (Eds.), Distributed, High-Performance and Grid Computing in Computational Biology. X, 192 pages. 2007. (Sublibrary LNBI).

Vol. 4358: R. Vidal, A. Heyden, Y. Ma (Eds.), Dynamical Vision. IX, 329 pages. 2007.

Vol. 4357: L. Buttyán, V. Gligor, D. Westhoff (Eds.), Security and Privacy in Ad-Hoc and Sensor Networks. X, 193 pages. 2006.

Vol. 4355: J. Julliand, O. Kouchnarenko (Eds.), B 2007: Formal Specification and Development in B. XIII, 293 pages. 2006.

Vol. 4354: M. Hanus (Ed.), Practical Aspects of Declarative Languages. X, 335 pages. 2006.

Vol. 4353: T. Schwentick, D. Suciu (Eds.), Database Theory – ICDT 2007. XI, 419 pages. 2006.

Vol. 4352: T.-J. Cham, J. Cai, C. Dorai, D. Rajan, T.-S. Chua, L.-T. Chia (Eds.), Advances in Multimedia Modeling, Part II. XVIII, 743 pages. 2006.

Vol. 4351: T.-J. Cham, J. Cai, C. Dorai, D. Rajan, T.-S. Chua, L.-T. Chia (Eds.), Advances in Multimedia Modeling, Part I. XIX, 797 pages. 2006.

Vol. 4349: B. Cook, A. Podelski (Eds.), Verification, Model Checking, and Abstract Interpretation. XI, 395 pages. 2007.

Vol. 4348: S.T. Taft, R.A. Duff, R.L. Brukardt, E. Ploedereder, P. Leroy (Eds.), Ada 2005 Reference Manual. XXII, 765 pages. 2006.

Vol. 4347: J. Lopez (Ed.), Critical Information Infrastructures Security. X, 286 pages. 2006.

Vol. 4346: L. Brim, B. Haverkort, M. Leucker, J. van de Pol (Eds.), Formal Methods: Applications and Technology. X, 363 pages. 2007.

Vol. 4345: N. Maglaveras, I. Chouvarda, V. Koutkias, R. Brause (Eds.), Biological and Medical Data Analysis. XIII, 496 pages. 2006. (Sublibrary LNBI).

Vol. 4344: V. Gruhn, F. Oquendo (Eds.), Software Architecture. X, 245 pages. 2006.

Lecture Notes in Computer Science

For information about Vols. 1–4342

please contact your bookseller or Springer

Vol. 4453: T. Speed, H. Huang (Eds.), Research in Computational Molecular Biology. XVI, 550 pages. 2007. (Sublibrary LNBI).

Vol. 4448: M. Giacobini (Ed.), Applications of Evolutionary Computing. XXIII, 755 pages. 2007.

Vol. 4447: E. Marchiori, J.H. Moore, J.C. Rajapakse (Eds.), Evolutionary Computation,Machine Learning and Data Mining in Bioinformatics. XI, 302 pages. 2007.

Vol. 4446: C. Cotta, J. van Hemert (Eds.), Evolutionary Computation in Combinatorial Optimization. XII, 241 pages. 2007.

Vol. 4445: M. Ebner, M. O'Neill, A. Ekárt, L. Vanneschi, A.I. Esparcia-Alcázar (Eds.), Genetic Programming. XI, 382 pages. 2007.

Vol. 4444: T. Reps, M. Sagiv, J. Bauer (Eds.), Program Analysis and Compilation, Theory and Practice. X, 361 pages. 2007.

Vol. 4443: R. Kotagiri, P.R. Krishna, M.K. Mohania, E. Nantajeewarawat (Eds.), Advances in Databases: Concepts, Systems and Applications. XXI, 1126 pages. 2007.

Vol. 4431: B. Beliczynski, A. Dzielinski, M. Iwanowski, B. Ribeiro (Eds.), Adaptive and Natural Computing Algorithms, Part I. XXV, 851 pages. 2007.

Vol. 4430: C.C. Yang, D. Zeng, M. Chau, K. Chang, Q. Yang, X. Cheng, J. Wang, F.-Y. Wang, H. Chen (Eds.), Intelligence and Security Informatics. XII, 330 pages. 2007.

Vol. 4429: R. Lu, J.H. Siekmann, C. Ullrich (Eds.), Cognitive Systems. X, 161 pages. 2007. (Sublibrary LNAI).

Vol. 4427: S. Uhlig, K. Papagiannaki, O. Bonaventure (Eds.), Passive and Active Network Measurement. XI, 274 pages. 2007.

Vol. 4425: G. Amati, C. Carpineto, G. Romano (Eds.), Advances in Information Retrieval. XIX, 759 pages. 2007.

Vol. 4424: O. Grumberg, M. Huth (Eds.), Tools and Algorithms for the Construction and Analysis of Systems. XX, 738 pages. 2007.

Vol. 4423: H. Seidl (Ed.), Foundations of Software Science and Computational Structures. XVI, 379 pages. 2007.

Vol. 4422: M.B. Dwyer, A. Lopes (Eds.), Fundamental Approaches to Software Engineering. XV, 440 pages. 2007.

Vol. 4421: R. De Nicola (Ed.), Programming Languages and Systems. XVII, 538 pages. 2007.

Vol. 4420: S. Krishnamurthi, M. Odersky (Eds.), Compiler Construction. XIV, 233 pages. 2007.

Vol. 4419: P.C. Diniz, E. Marques, K. Bertels, M.M. Fernandes, J.M.P. Cardoso (Eds.), Reconfigurable Computing: Architectures, Tools and Applications. XIV, 391 pages. 2007.

Vol. 4418: A. Gagalowicz, W. Philips (Eds.), Computer Vision/Computer Graphics Collaboration Techniques. XV, 620 pages. 2007.

Vol. 4416: A. Bemporad, A. Bicchi, G. Buttazzo (Eds.), Hybrid Systems: Computation and Control. XVII, 797 pages. 2007.

Vol. 4415: P. Lukowicz, L. Thiele, G. Tröster (Eds.), Architecture of Computing Systems - ARCS 2007. X, 297 pages. 2007.

Vol. 4414: S. Hochreiter, R. Wagner (Eds.), Bioinformatics Research and Development. XVI, 482 pages. 2007. (Sublibrary LNBI).

Vol. 4412: F. Stajano, H.J. Kim, J.-S. Chae, S.-D. Kim (Eds.), Ubiquitous Convergence Technology. XI, 302 pages. 2007.

Vol. 4410: A. Branco (Ed.), Anaphora: Analysis, Algorithms and Applications. X, 191 pages. 2007. (Sublibrary LNAI).

Vol. 4407: G. Puebla (Ed.), Logic-Based Program Synthesis and Transformation. VIII, 237 pages. 2007.

Vol. 4406: W. De Meuter (Ed.), Advances in Smalltalk. VII, 157 pages. 2007.

Vol. 4405: L. Padgham, F. Zambonelli (Eds.), Agent-Oriented Software Engineering VII. XII, 225 pages. 2007.

Vol. 4403: S. Obayashi, K. Deb, C. Poloni, T. Hiroyasu, T. Murata (Eds.), Evolutionary Multi-Criterion Optimization. XIX, 954 pages. 2007.

Vol. 4400: J.F. Peters, A. Skowron, V.W. Marek, E. Orłowska, R. Slowinski, W. Ziarko (Eds.), Transactions on Rough Sets VII, Part II. X, 381 pages. 2007.

Vol. 4399: T. Kovacs, X. Llorà, K. Takadama, P.L. Lanzi, W. Stolzmann, S.W. Wilson (Eds.), Learning Classifier Systems. XII, 345 pages. 2007. (Sublibrary LNAI).

Vol. 4398: S. Marchand-Maillet, E. Bruno, A. Nürnberger, M. Detyniecki (Eds.), Adaptive Multimedia Retrieval: User, Context, and Feedback. XI, 269 pages. 2007.

Vol. 4397: C. Stephanidis, M. Pieper (Eds.), Universal Access in Ambient Intelligence Environments. XV, 467 pages. 2007.

Vol. 4396: J. García-Vidal, L. Cerdà-Alabern (Eds.), Wireless Systems and Mobility in Next Generation Internet. IX, 271 pages. 2007.